W9-ASQ-812

FRENCH GENERAL

# HANDMADE SOIRÉES

FRENCH GENERAL

# HANDMADE SOIRÉES

SIMPLE
PROJECTS FOR SPECIAL
OCCASIONS

BY KAARI MENG
PHOTOGRAPHS BY JON ZABALA

CHRONICLE BOOKS
SAN FRANCISCO

Text copyright © 2009 by Kaari Meng.
Photographs copyright © 2009 by Jon Zabala.
Illustrations copyright © 2009 by Jody Rice.

All rights reserved. No part of this book may be reproduced in any
form without written permission from the publisher.

Library of Congress Cataloging-in-Publication Data:
Meng, Kaari. French General: Handmade Soirées: simple
projects for special occasions /
by Kaari Meng; photographs by Jon Zabala.
p. cm. Includes index.
ISBN-13: 978-0-8118-6833-4
1. Table setting and decoration. 2. Entertaining. 3. Handicraft. I. Title.
TX879.M45 2009  642'.6—dc22  2008048125

Manufactured in China
Designed by River Jukes-Hudson

10 9 8 7 6 5 4 3 2 1

FolkArt and Mod Podge are registered trademarks
of Plaid Enterprises, Inc.
X-Acto is a registered trademark of Elmer's Products, Inc.

Chronicle Books LLC
680 Second Street
San Francisco, California 94107

www.chroniclebooks.com

TO FRIENDS AND FAMILY WHO HAVE TAUGHT ME TO
CREATE, COOK, AND CELEBRATE.

# TABLE OF CONTENTS

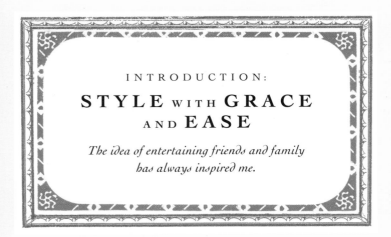

# STYLE WITH GRACE AND EASE

*The idea of entertaining friends and family
has always inspired me.*

I have always enjoyed the details involved with planning a meal and having friends over to share. I like the ideas that surface when you start to think about inviting people into your home. Who you can entertain, when you can entertain, why you entertain. The possibilities are endless, and I think part of the fun of entertaining is making these creative decisions while planning the event. It's a creative process that I enjoy. When I was young, I ran a party-planning business with a best friend who lived down the street. We organized small gatherings for children under six—we were only ten. From picking out the color of the napkins to handwriting the invitations, I was into it.

I still love all the rituals involved in entertaining: writing the guest list, making the invitations, deciding on what to eat and drink, setting the table, creating the atmosphere around the occasion, and, finally, serving the meal itself—gathering with people who make you feel good inside and give you a bit of themselves when you get together. When I was growing up, my parents invited friends over for any celebration we could think of. Once an idea for a party emerged, we would all get to work planning the event.

When I lived in New York, my friends and I enjoyed throwing small, elegant dinner parties. It was always the same group of us: eight people who loved setting a table with all of our flea-market finds...flatware, glassware, plates, and linens. We usually spent the day of the meal collecting fresh food, dusting off our unchipped serving pieces, and making sure there was plenty of good Scotch for the after-dinner party. The meals would start early and go late into the night. I learned that oversize white linen napkins are best; scented candles do not belong on the dining table; and in order to truly enjoy haggis, you must serve it with a Robert Burns poem—all essential entertaining skills. The little details from these simple, intimate meals we shared remain a part of my entertaining repertoire today.

Over the years, I have collected ideas for entertaining from friends, good restaurants, and even the sausage cart at the flea market in Toulouse. There are always fun, new ways of bringing people together to eat. For this book, we came up with some of our favorites and then added in a couple more creative nights. At our Harvest Dinner (see page 126), we served escargots and boudin noir (blood sausages) at a wooden thrasher's table in our garage. We had an exposed brick wall and thought it made a suitable background for a country meal. As always, the best entertaining is born from starting with what you have and adding a special touch.

The atmosphere you create for your meal should always bring about a sense of peace and unity—gathering different friends together and feeding them is a way of keeping everyone connected. Have fun with the food

you prepare. Serve what you are comfortable cooking and then try something new once in a while just to mix things up a bit. There is a lot to be said for old favorites—friends will always appreciate tasting recipes that have been in your family for years. Our Moule Frites Fête (see page 82) was a first ever—a learning experience. I learned how to cook mussels with a bottle of wine, a large handful of chopped garlic, and a whole lot of butter. The leftover broth made a four-star pasta sauce!

Although many people think food is the main event at a meal, setting a well-thought-out, creative table creates a welcoming atmosphere for your friends. This is when there are no recipes—anything goes. For Sofia's tea party with Gracie (see page 32), I pulled out all of my old pink luster teacups and saucers. I dug up some cranberry glasses that I had bought years ago in London and a couple of old ruby red finger bowls. Small cake plates were used to display the petite sweets, and name cards were set just for the fun of it. We made party favors that turned into a delightful game, and we hung embellished lanterns for the festivities. Adding in your own personal touch is your gift to your guests. If time is short, a hand-stamped paper plate serves as a simple but always thoughtful place setting. At the end of the day, the most important part of entertaining is bringing people together for stimulating conversation, laughter, and lasting memories. Whenever I visit Paris, my roommate from college, Dominique, puts on a fabulous meal in her apartment and invites friends she would like me to meet. The food is served in different courses, and between each course she gives people time to talk and learn about each other. By the end of the meal I feel as if I am sitting with friends I have known forever. Learning to entertain is understanding how to balance the people with the food and the décor. Spend a little time planning out your event and you will be able to relax and enjoy the meal with your guests.

Throughout this book, I offer examples of how I set our family tables and the food we serve when we get together on special occasions. I've also created some fun and simple crafts that can add a little extra zip to your next party. Try the painted lanterns (see page 44) and hang them over your table any time there is a fancy gathering. As a hostess gift, hand-stitch a collection of cocktail napkins (see page 46) using recycled fabric to create a special memory. Set your table with some homemade and some well-worn materials, and you will have created a lovely environment to entertain your friends and family in.

## COLLECTING
# TABLE OBJECTS

*Because I cannot pass up a good flea market,
estate sale, or thrift shop, I tend to dig quite hard for
my entertaining tabletop pieces.*

Much of my entertaining collection comes from my parents' house—the classic Scandinavian enameled bowls, my dad's collection of low-ball monogrammed glasses, and the Swedish crystal decanters. These pieces mix in well with my own collection of early American and French pieces. Clean lines, good shape, and a bit of the odd and unusual somehow blend together to make my own personal table style.

Finding your table style—learning what you like and don't like—takes a bit of practice. You may have a full set of china dishes from your grandmother that you save for special occasions—why not pull out the salad plates for a special dessert some night? Or make a custom set of napkin rings to match your dinnerware? These small touches will not go unnoticed.

There are some basics to follow as you collect, but really the possibilities are endless. Plates, glassware, napkins, and flatware have been around for hundreds of years, and the designs range from very simple to highly decorative. I find that if an item is useful I need it, but if the item is also beautiful then I want it. Setting your table with items that resonate with you and that make you happy, for whatever reason, is usually a good way to start collecting.

Once your entertaining collection is under way, you can slowly build it by adding favorite pieces every now and then. If you have a large family and love to serve family-style, then collecting platters should be at the top of your list. If you love wine-tasting evenings, then be sure to look for small carafes to offer a flight of wine to your guests. Half the fun of entertaining is using some of these special pieces that you wouldn't normally use on a regular basis.

If you find yourself hunting through secondhand, antique, or used shops, here are some ideas to keep in mind for your entertaining repertoire.

### ·❧GLASSWARE❧·

When collecting glassware, it is always best to start with pieces in good condition: no chips or cracks. Look for unusually shaped glasses used to serve different types of drinks—there are hundreds of styles. I think the shape of a glass makes a difference in the enjoyment of your drink. Drinking water out of an old water goblet reminds me to drink more water. Have fun with colored glassware. My favorite is cranberry glass—it gives off a soft, golden glow around candles. Think about what drinks you serve most often. If you love champagne, build up your collection of flutes. If you typically entertain more casually, look for low, straight,

stemless glasses, which are commonly used to serve table wine in France. Finding full sets of vintage or old glassware can be quite rare, so consider collecting a certain shape glass—your collection will become eclectic and fun. Cleaning your glassware by hand is usually best—and you won't have to worry about any hard-water spots if you dry it by hand. A soft sponge, soapy water, and a linen towel are all you need.

## ·❀CHINA❀·

I have a weakness for plates—even tiny doll plates. I look for china or porcelain plates in different sizes so that they can be used for serving food as well as for place settings. Old saucers that have lost their tea-cups are perfect for serving jam or butter on. When looking for vintage plates and platters, use the no-chip rule, as a small chip can usually lead to a larger crack. Solid-colored plates are always useful and don't distract from the food. Early ironstone plates are a good basic plate to start collecting. The creamy white ironstone plates are durable and simple enough for everyday use. Once you have built up a collection of your dinner plates, look for a complementary set of salad plates that you can set on top of or alongside your dinner plates. I tend to collect more salad plates so that I can switch them out depending upon the meal. Store your plates with a paper plate tucked in between each one to prevent them from scratching.

## ·❀FLATWARE❀·

Small, portable, and relatively cheap to collect, good old silver-plate flatware sets a wonderful table, either fancy or plain. Finding a complete set of old flatware is never easy. Look for handles that you like and make up your own sets. Before you buy, test out the tongs on forks and the blades on knives to be sure that they are still somewhat sharp. Half the fun of collecting flatware is taking it home and polishing it. The details and etchings on old silver plate are usually crystal clear once cleaned with a soft sponge and silver polish. I love early coin-silver spoons crafted from silver melted down from coins. You can usually spot them by the pure silver color and light weight. They make for particularly elegant serving spoons. Small, decorative serving pieces with mother-of-pearl handles are perfect for tea parties or smaller tables. Hand-washing the mother-of-pearl and storing the utensils in a soft cutlery roll will preserve the handles for years to come.

## · LINEN ·

Linen, my favorite, is the most fun to collect. Opera-size linen napkins, tablecloths with hand-embroidered red monograms, and rustic hemp runners all help soften the table. Used together, they add layers to the table settings and give the occasion a rich, historical, and comfortable feeling. When you start collecting your table linens, think about color and texture. What color are your plates? What color are the walls? Let your linen collection tie the room together with your tabletop collection. So many of my table linens have been repurposed from other household textiles. A less-than-perfect linen tablecloth can be cut up and sewn into napkins. Tea towels make great placemats. Wash and wear is important with the linens. Spot treat any stains as soon as you can to keep linens clean. When your linens are starting to show years of being laundered, think about dying them a darker color for a fresh new start.

CREATING AN

**ATMOSPHERE**

COLOR

*plays a big part in setting my tables.*

———

Making a conscientious choice about color can bring all the elements together, even the eclectic ones, which is key for entertaining with a mix-and-match style collection. I love playing with color palettes to see how they will interact with each other. Natural linens are a subtle way to allow the textures to come through in your table setting. Whether it is an elegant or rustic table, the tonal colors of oyster, sand, and ivory—such as those used in the Midsummer's Eve table (see page 112)—can lend a delicate balance and allow you to use a variety of serving pieces without seeming random. Sometimes bringing in a unique color, like the teal-dyed hemp sheet we used for the fabric banners at our Poolside Grill Dinner (see page 108), adds instant atmosphere. Adding a shock of color makes the event seem festive and fun and gives you a chance to bring out all of your mismatched china and glassware.

I always think it's easiest to start with the linens, because they often make the biggest impression. The palette for each of the tables in this book always began with the textiles—a faded linen floral tablecloth or an aubergine sheet, for example—and then we added our plates, glassware, and flatware to layer the table. Deciding what to mix with your fabric color choice is when the blending of the soft and the hard elements come together. For our Petite Déjeuner table (see page 16), I liked the freshness of the French red tablecloth mixed with the creamy ironstone plates and breakfast bowls. In planning out each event, we wanted the table settings to be well balanced, interesting, and inviting.

Once a table has been anchored with my favorite linens and pieces, I like to add little surprises that make my friends feel welcome and special. Candles and music are always at the top of my list for hosting an evening affair. Setting out name cards (see pages 33 and 74) creates excitement for guests to sit near someone they might not have met before. Napkin rings (see page 128) add a bit of old-world charm to your table and also let people stash their own napkin for the next meal. A handwritten menu board (see page 71) lets everyone know what the chef has been busy preparing throughout the day. Cutting fresh flowers and arranging a small vase (see page 137) at each table setting allows your friends to take home a small memento of the meal.

Spending a bit of time on the atmosphere creates a warm event that feels inviting and comfortable. I hope in this book you find a few fresh ways to personalize your own tables. Have some fun with your own entertaining style, and your guests will love coming back to your table to dine.

# PETITE DÉJEUNER

*An early-morning breakfast needs to be fresh and calming.*

———————————

THIS IS THE MEAL THAT WILL SET YOUR TONE FOR THE DAY. BY KEEPING EVERYTHING EASY, YOU ALLOW YOURSELF TO ENJOY THE FIRST FEW HOURS OF THE DAY. I LIKE TAKING THE TIME TO LAY OUT AN INVITING TABLE THAT USES SOME OF MY PRETTY FRENCH BREAKFAST PIECES—BREAKFAST BOWLS FOR COFFEE, IRONSTONE PLATES, AND LINEN CLOTHS. ✳ IN RURAL FRANCE, EACH TOWN HAS ITS OWN LOCAL BOULANGER THAT SERVES UP FRESH CROISSANTS, BAGUETTES, AND BRIOCHE AT THE CRACK OF DAWN. WHOEVER IS UP FIRST IN THE HOUSE IS USUALLY THE DESIGNATED BREAD FETCHER—AND THE BAGUETTES VERY OFTEN COME HOME WITH THE TOP EATEN OFF. WHO CAN RESIST FRESH BREAD? IN CALIFORNIA, I HAVE GOTTEN USED TO PICKING UP THE BREAD THE DAY BEFORE AND THEN WARMING IT IN THE OVEN FOR A COUPLE OF MINUTES BEFORE SERVING IT. ACCOMPANIED BY FRE   BUTTER AND HOMEMADE JAM, IT IS ALWAYS EVERYONE'S FAVORITE. ❧

# CUP OF COFFEE

*To make the perfect cup of coffee at home, start with freshly ground medium-roast coffee, filtered water, and a clean French coffee press.*

**ADD 1 SCOOP OF GROUND COFFEE FOR EACH CUP.**

Pour boiling water into the coffee press and stir with a wooden spoon to mix all the coffee grounds thoroughly.

Let steep for at least 5 to 8 minutes and then slowly push down on the top of the plunger to press the coffee grounds to the bottom of the glass carafe.

**POUR THE COFFEE INTO HEAT-RETAINING IRONSTONE OR CERAMIC CUPS.**

*Coffee this good needs to be served with fresh whole milk or cream and a natural sweetener such as honey or organic sugar.*

# EMBROIDERED JAM COVERS

*Top off your homemade, or even store-bought, gourmet jam with these charming embroidered linen covers. At the back of this book we've included the designs for our favorite toppers, though you could always embroider an initial, which would work on any type of jar. Be sure to make a few extra, as these make thoughtful gifts you'll always be happy to have on hand. This is a great project to use up your small fabric scraps—and if you are short on time, you could stamp out the name of the jam with fabric ink and rubber stamps.*

## MATERIALS (FOR ONE JAM COVER)

¼ YARD (23 CM) BROWN LINEN

EMBROIDERY FLOSS IN ASSORTED COLORS

EMBROIDERY NEEDLE

EMBROIDERY SCISSORS

IRON

PENCIL

36" (91.4 CM) NARROW RIBBON

NOTE: The directions below are for jam jars with mouths that are 3" (7.62 cm) to 3½" (8.9 cm) in diameter. You may want to increase or decrease the size of the designs and the circle you cut in step 2, depending on the size of your jars.

## DIRECTIONS

**1.** Using the designs provided at the back of the book (see page 146), transfer the one you wish to use onto the linen. Embroider the design using the stitches listed in the General Techniques section, or however you wish.

**2.** Cut the fabric to an 8" (20.3 cm) circle, with the embroidered design in the center.

**3.** With your fingers, press under ⅛" (32 mm) all the way around the circle. Finish the edge by hand using a blanket stitch.

**4.** Mark eight evenly spaced eyelets around the cover, about 1" (2.54 cm) from the finished edge, drawing a circle about the size of a pencil eraser for each.

**5.** To make an eyelet by hand, first stitch around the marked circle using a running stitch. Then, using very small, sharp embroidery scissors, cut a hole just inside the stitched circle. Using a pencil or your fingers, gently turn the cut edge to the **Wrong** side. Finish by doing a small satin stitch all the way around the hole, completely covering the previous stitches.

**6.** Alternatively, you can make buttonholes on a sewing machine or use metal eyelets.

**7.** Thread a narrow ribbon through all the eyelets and then back in the other direction until you reach where you started. Place the cover on a jam jar and cinch the ribbon to fit.

# EGG BERETS

*I learned early on that getting Sofia to eat eggs in the morning was easier if we made eggs and soldiers. Simply soft-boil a couple of eggs and cut your toast into strips for the soldiers. For a bit more whimsy, make these easy berets to place on top of your soft-boiled eggs. Just for fun, let your guest give the petite* oeuf *a mustache with a small brush and a bit of coffee.* Voilà!

## MATERIALS (FOR SIX BERETS)

ONE 9" x 12" (23 x 30 CM) PIECE RED CRAFT FELT

RED THREAD

HAND-SEWING NEEDLE

CRAFT GLUE

6 SMALL RED POM-POMS

FOOD COLORING OR STRONG BLACK COFFEE

SMALL PAINTBRUSH

SCISSORS

## DIRECTIONS (FOR ONE BERET)

**1.** Using the pattern provided at the back of the book (see page 146), cut out one beret crown and one beret brim out of felt.

**2.** With **Right** sides together, hand-sew the brim and crown together around the outside edge using a very small whipstitch.

**3.** Turn the beret **Right** side out. Glue a pom-pom to the top of the hat. Using your fingers, gently stretch the inside of the hat until it fits snugly on an egg.

**4.** Using strong coffee or food coloring, paint a mustache on your egg.

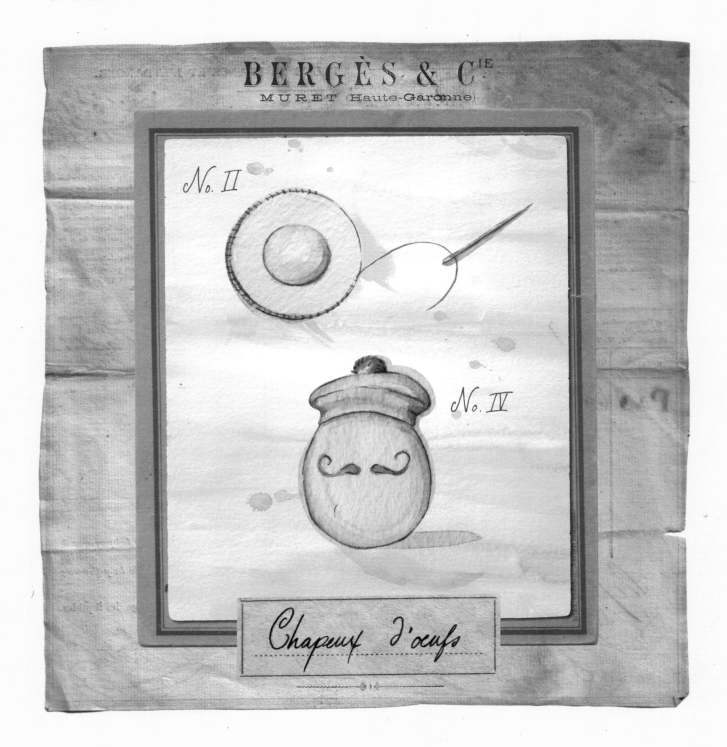

# FABRIC-COVERED RECIPE BOX

*My mom has always had hundreds of recipes floating around the kitchen. This fabric-covered recipe box is a useful and pretty heirloom gift for all of your friends who love to cook. Since so little fabric is needed, dip into your most treasured old fabric collection to make the box extra special. Embellish index cards with a simple border, and include some of your prized family recipes inside of the box.*

## MATERIALS (FOR ONE BOX)

WOODEN RECIPE BOX (OR ANY BOX WITH A LID)

ACRYLIC PAINT

SMALL PAINTBRUSHES

FABRIC SCRAPS (ABOUT ¼ YARD, OR 23 CM TOTAL)

X-ACTO KNIFE

DECOUPAGE MEDIUM, SUCH AS MOD PODGE

EXTRA-FINE SANDPAPER (OPTIONAL)

PAPER FOR MAKING A PATTERN

PENCIL

## DIRECTIONS

**1.** Remove any hardware from your box, such as the hinges.

**2.** Make a paper pattern for the fabric pieces you will be applying to the box by tracing or measuring all the sides. The pattern should fit exactly without any overlap. Try to make your pattern using as few pieces as possible—we covered our boxes using only one piece of fabric for the box and another for the lid.

**3.** Paint the inside of the box and lid with acrylic paint. (We used FolkArt paint in Buttercup.) Apply several coats and let dry completely.

**4.** Trace your pattern onto the **Wrong** side of the fabric. Using an X-Acto knife, carefully cut out your pieces, making your edges as clean as possible.

**5.** Following the directions on your decoupage medium, apply the fabric to the box and lid. If your fabric stretches a bit as you apply it, don't worry. Once the first coat is dry, you can trim any ragged edges with the X-Acto knife.

**6.** Continue applying coats of the medium until you are happy with the result. Once you have built up enough coats, you may lightly sand any bumps or bubbles that have appeared, then apply another coat.

**7.** Reattach the hardware.

# TEA FLOWER PARTY

*Throwing an afternoon tea party using your favorite old dishes and*
*teacups can be an escape into make-believe,*
*as it is for my daughter, Sofia, and her friend Gracie.*

———————

PULL OUT YOUR OLD SET OF TEACUPS AND SAUCERS OR MIX AND MATCH YOUR FAVORITE ONES. USE SMALLER PLATES AND CUPS SO THAT EVERYTHING CAN BE HELD BY LITTLE HANDS. TEA PARTIES ARE THE PERFECT SMALL FANCY EVENT, SO BE SURE TO USE YOUR PRETTIEST TEAPOT, SUGAR SPOONS, AND CAKE PLATES. ❋ SWEET TREATS AND SAVORY SANDWICHES ARE A NICE COMBINATION FOR LITTLE APPETITES. LOOK FOR A LOCAL BAKERY THAT MAKES PETITE TREATS, SUCH AS SCONES OR MUFFINS, LEMON CAKES, AND BONBONS. SERVE THESE SWEETS WITH A SELECTION OF TEA SANDWICHES MADE THE DAY OF THE PARTY. SOFIA ENJOYS MAKING TRIANGLE-CUT SANDWICHES FILLED WITH FINE SLICES OF CUCUMBER AND RADISHES OR HAM AND FRESH BUTTER. ❧

*Kaari*

*Gracie*

*Sofia*

*Molly*

## COLLECTING
# YOUR FAVORITE COLOR

*Flea markets, estate sales,
and thrift shops
can sometimes be overwhelming.
To make your shopping easier, try picking
a color you would like to collect for
your tableware, then look at everything
in that color—glassware,
china, enamel platters, flatware
handles, and linens.*

Once I settle on a tableware color to collect, I am able to pick out special pieces in a sea of collectibles. Choosing a color can be as easy as picking what you like, what blends with what you already have, or, if you are lucky, finding a color that no one else is collecting! I tend to collect cranberry glass and pink luster ironstone. I look for any shade from petal pink to ruby red and then mix them all together—somehow they are eclectic enough to blend together and not look too precious.

# FLORAL LANTERNS

*Create a sweet spot in a room with decorated lanterns. Paint plain paper lanterns with an arborous design and attach petals cut out from tissue paper, or look for old millinery flowers in shades of pink and coral. For vintage charm and whimsy, hang the lanterns from the ceiling with silk ribbon. If your table already has a hanging light or chandelier above it, try making a garland of old millinery flowers strung together with beads as accent pieces.*

## MATERIALS

ASSORTED PAPER LANTERNS (WE USED WHITE GLOBES 6", 8", AND 12" IN (15.2, 20.3, AND 30.5 CM) DIAMETER)

PAINTBRUSH

ACRYLIC PAINT IN OFF-WHITE (OPTIONAL)

TISSUE PAPER IN ASSORTED SHADES OF PINK

SCISSORS

MINI STAPLER

CRAFT GLUE

WATERCOLOR PAINTS IN ASSORTED SHADES OF GREEN

GOLD SEQUINS OR BEADS

## DIRECTIONS

**1.** If your lanterns are bright white, start by "antiquing" them by painting on a thin wash of off-white paint.

**2.** While the lanterns are drying, assemble the paper flowers. To make one flower, cut two large petals and two small petals out of tissue paper using the templates provided in the back of the book (see page 150). Staple the layers together in the center, with the small petals on top. Using your fingers, curl the edges of the petals to "fluff" them up. We used six flowers for the 6" (15.2 cm) lantern, eight flowers for the 8" (20.3 cm) lantern, and twelve flowers for the 12" (30.5 cm) lantern.

**3.** Glue the flowers to your lantern with craft glue.

**4.** Using green watercolors, paint a vine and leaves around the lantern, connecting the flowers.

**5.** Cover the stapled flower centers by gluing sequins or beads to each flower.

No. II          4 layers

No. IV

Lanterne de Fleur

# MONOGRAMMED NAPKINS

*Sew up a set of linen napkins or find an old set at the flea market and embroider each guest's initial with some bright-colored floss. Use these pretty napkins over and over, or let each guest take one home as a special gift. Take advantage of our decorative alphabet (see page 148) for your monograms, or easily create your own letters by stamping the guest's initials with rubber stamps and ink and then stitching over them. To complete the look, try making simple napkin rings using a bit of ribbon and some pretty old millinery buds and leaves.*

## MATERIALS

WHITE LINEN NAPKINS, ABOUT 14" (36 CM) SQUARE

EMBROIDERY FLOSS IN ASSORTED COLORS

EMBROIDERY NEEDLE

## DIRECTIONS

**1.** Make or buy white linen napkins.

**2.** Using the alphabet provided in the back of the book (see page 148), transfer the desired letter to one corner of your napkin.

**3.** Fill in the solid areas of the design using a satin stitch. To achieve the raised effect popular in old monograms, first outline the area to be filled using a split stitch. Then work the satin stitch, covering the outline.

**4.** Use a stem stitch on the vines in the design, and finish with a French knot in the center flower.

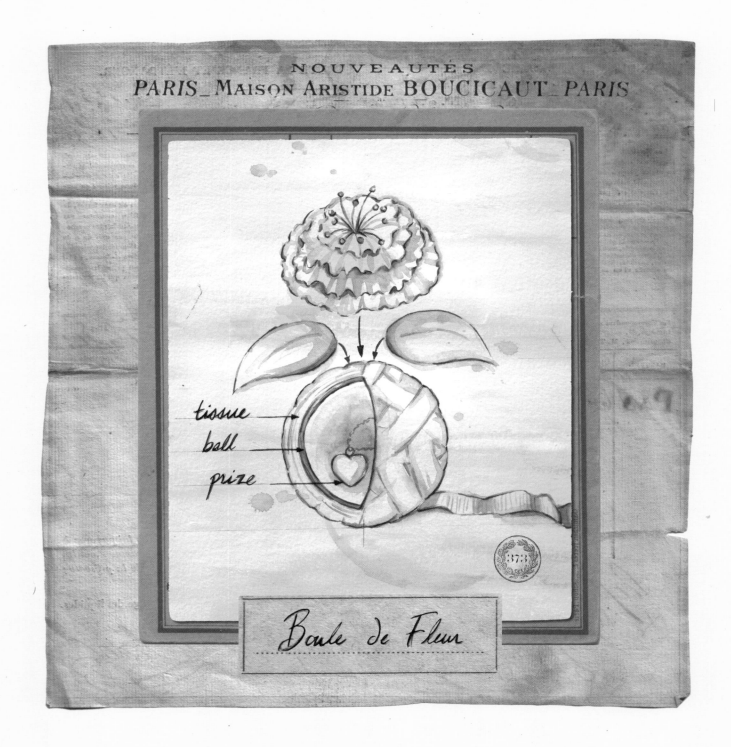

# FLOWER FAVORS

*Giving small party gifts to each of your guests turns into a "ball" of fun with these flower favors. Before wrapping each ball with strips of crepe paper, fill the ball with a surprise. Look for small trinkets or craft simple bracelets with charms to place inside each favor ball. Unraveling the crepe paper that covers the favor is as much fun as receiving the trinkets hidden inside.*

## MATERIALS (FOR ONE FAVOR)

HOLLOW CRAFT BALL ORNAMENT, ABOUT 3" (7.62 CM) IN DIAMETER (FOUND AT MOST CRAFT STORES)

SAW OR SHARP KNIFE

ACRYLIC PAINT AND PAINTBRUSH (OPTIONAL)

TRINKETS TO PUT INSIDE FAVOR

1" (2.54 CM)-WIDE CREPE PAPER STREAMERS IN ASSORTED SHADES OF PINK (IF STREAMERS ARE WIDER, CUT IN HALF)

CRAFT GLUE

TISSUE PAPER IN ASSORTED SHADES OF PINK AND GREEN

THIN FLORIST WIRE

CRAFT FLOWER STAMENS

PINKING SHEARS OR CRAFT SCISSORS

## DIRECTIONS

1. Carefully cut the ball in half using a saw or sharp knife, leaving a ½" (1.3 cm) section uncut as a "hinge" to keep the two halves connected. You may paint the ball or leave it unfinished. Place your favor trinkets inside and close the ball.

2. Begin wrapping crepe paper streamers around the ball until it is totally covered, alternating colors as you go. The more you wrap, the more fun it is to unwrap!

3. Secure the end of the last streamer to the ball with a drop of craft glue.

4. Start the flower by cutting out a piece 5" (12.7 cm) wide by 12" (30.4 cm) long through five layers of the pink tissue paper. Fold the stack of tissue paper accordion-style in ½" folds. Wrap a 4" (10.2 cm) piece of florist wire around the center of the folded piece, twisting it once to secure it in place.

5. Lay six flower stamens along the center of the folded stack, and wrap the wire around again, securing the stamens to the center. Trim the ends of the florist wire. Cut the ends of the folded stack of tissue paper, rounding off the corners so it resembles a popsicle stick.

6. Fan out the folds, and carefully begin pulling the layers apart, forming the flower. Bend flower stamens up toward the center of your flower.

7. Cut out several leaf shapes from the green tissue paper. Use pinking shears or other craft scissors to achieve a frilled edge. Glue the leaves to the underside of your flower.

8. Glue the flower to the favor ball.

# AFTERNOON PIQUE-NIQUE

*Once in a while I get the urge to eat outside—and not just eat outside, but live outside.*

I GREW UP CAMPING, LEARNING HOW TO ENJOY FOOD THAT WAS PRE-PREPARED AND MADE TO TRAVEL. THE WHOLE IDEA BEHIND THE FRENCH *PIQUE-NIQUE* IS TO ENTERTAIN FRIENDS AND FAMILY IN A VERY CASUAL, EASY MANNER. SANDWICHES ARE MADE THE NIGHT BEFORE SO THAT THE MEATS AND CHEESES HAVE A CHANCE TO BLEND. SALADS ARE A BIT HEARTIER, AND, MADE THE DAY BEFORE, THE OIL AND VINEGAR SOAKS INTO THE ELEMENTS FOR MORE FLAVOR. REFRESHING DRINKS QUENCH EVERYONE'S THIRST, AND A GOOD, HOMEMADE DESSERT SATISFIES THE SWEET TOOTH. �֍ MAKING YOUR PICNIC AS COMFORTABLE AS POSSIBLE WILL ENSURE THAT YOUR FRIENDS WILL LINGER AND RELAX FOR THE WHOLE DAY, RATHER THAN FOR JUST A MEAL. I LIKE TO BRING ALONG A LARGE PICNIC BLANKET—AN OLD SHEET, BED COVER, OR EVEN A QUILT—THAT WE CAN LAY OUT ON THE GROUND WITHOUT WORRYING ABOUT DIRTYING OR DAMAGING IT. THEN I LAYER THE PICNIC BLANKET WITH KING-SIZE PILLOWS THAT HAVE BEEN COVERED IN OLD TICKING MATERIAL—REDS AND BLUES ARE NICE BECAUSE THEY TEND NOT TO SHOW THE DIRT TOO QUICKLY. THINK ABOUT HANGING A SHEET OVERHEAD TO CREATE A LITTLE SHADE—THIS WILL ALLOW YOU TO RELAX WHILE EATING AND THEN ENCOURAGE THE OBLIGATORY POSTPICNIC NAP. ❧

# WOVEN BASKETS

I am always on the lookout for the perfect basket—a beautiful, handwoven container that will help me carry my goods from one place to another. Sometimes I find small baskets without handles—these are ideal for storing napkin rings, napkins, and even flatware. Larger baskets, with handles intact, are perfect for carrying food or picking up groceries at your local farmers' market.

Consider sewing a liner into some of your favorite baskets to protect the contents. You can also add a drawstring liner for more protection. I like to sew my liners out of hemp because the natural fibers resist dirt and dry quickly when washed. If you find a well-worn basket in need of a wash, simply give it a quick spray with a garden hose and let it sit outside to dry. Treat your basket collection well by storing baskets in a cool, dry place where they won't be exposed to moisture.

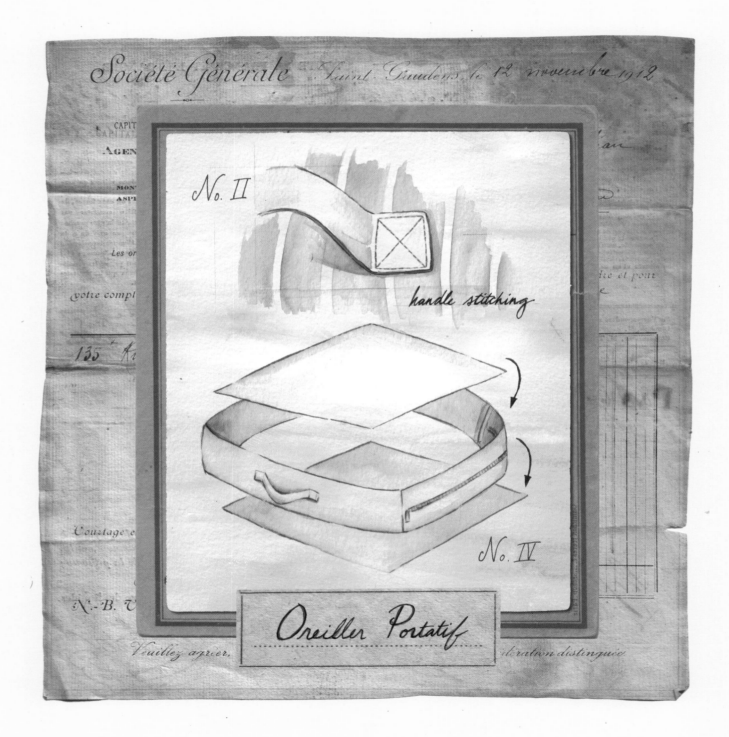

# CARRY CUSHION

*If you want to make your picnic extra comfortable, sew up a few of these cushions with fabric handles for easy carrying. Use durable fabric that will hold up to the dirt that is sure to appear after a picnic in the field. We used a ticking on one side and natural hemp on the other for versatility. When they're not out for afternoon picnics, you can use these cushions on your garden furniture.*

## MATERIALS

1 YARD (60" WIDE) BLUE TICKING

2/3 YARD (45" WIDE) (60 CM, 114 CM WIDE) NATURAL HEMP

SCISSORS

SEWING MACHINE

IRON

22" (56 CM) ZIPPER

20" x 20" x 4" (51 x 51 x 10 CM) PILLOW FORM OR FOAM

## DIRECTIONS

**1.** Cut one 21" (53 cm) square out of the blue ticking and another 21" (53 cm) square out of the hemp. Then cut one 58"-by-5" (147 x 13 cm) strip and two 23"-by-3" (58 x 8 cm) strips out of the blue ticking. For the handle, cut two 10"-by-1½" (25 x 4 cm) strips out of the blue ticking.

**2.** To make the handle, sew the handle pieces down the long edges, **Right** sides together, using a ¼" (6 cm) seam allowance. Turn **Right** side out and press. Then press each short edge under ½" (1.3 cm). Center the handle about 10½" (26.7 cm) from one end of the long ticking strip. Topstitch the pressed ends in place, making a 1" (2.5 cm) box. Stitch across the diagonals of the box as well.

**3.** Install the zipper between the two shorter ticking strips using a ½" (1.3 cm) seam allowance. Sew the zippered piece to the long strip, making one continuous circle.

**4.** Centering the zipper along one edge, sew the strip to the hemp square, **Right** sides together, using a ½" (1.3 cm) seam allowance. Clip into the seam allowance on the strip to fit around the corners of the square.

**5.** Open the zipper and repeat step 4 with the ticking square. Trim the corners and turn **Right** side out. Stuff with the pillow form or a foam square.

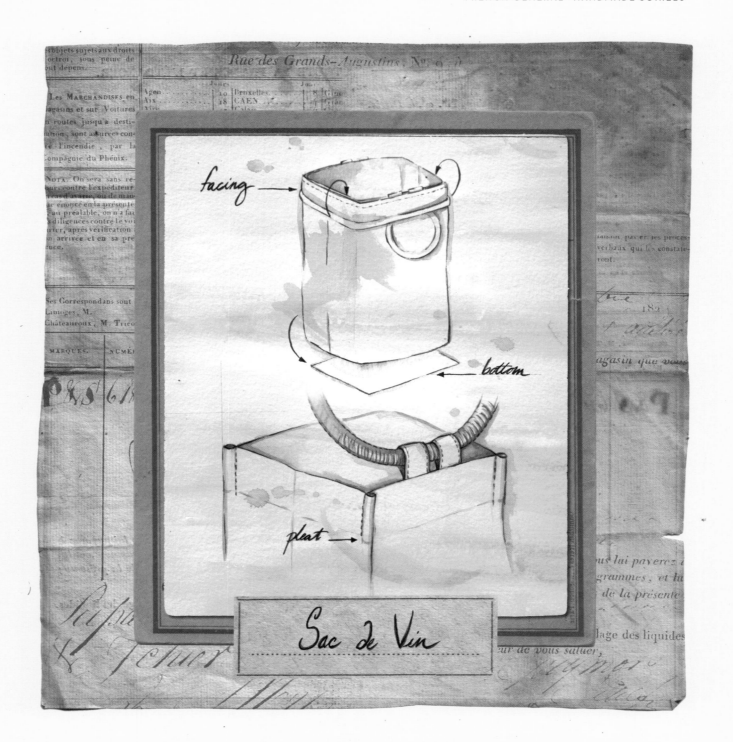

facing

bottom

pleat

Sac de Vin

# WINE TOTE

*Carrying your favorite beverage to a picnic can be made easy with this elegant tote bag. Sewn out of hemp and fashioned with handles, we stamped this tote with one of our favorite vintages. You can make up one of your own designs or use our template at the back of the book (see page 163). Be sure to use a durable fabric and handles so that they can withstand the weight of the bottle you are carrying. A votre santé!*

## MATERIALS

½ YARD (45" WIDE) (46 CM, 114 CM WIDE) NATURAL HEMP

SCISSORS

TRANSFER PAPER

BROWN FABRIC PAINT

SMALL PAINTBRUSH

SEWING MACHINE

IRON

WOOD OR BAMBOO PURSE HANDLES, 4" (10.2 CM) TO 5" (12.7 CM) IN DIAMETER

## DIRECTIONS

**1.** Out of the hemp, cut two rectangles 13" (33 cm) long by 9" (23 cm) wide (sides), one 4½" (11.4 cm) square (bottom), one strip 17" (43.2 cm) long by 2½" (6.3 cm) wide (facing), and two strips 16" (40.6 cm) long by 1½" (3.8 cm) wide (tabs).

**2.** Using the image provided, transfer the design onto one of the 13"-by-9" (33 x 23 cm) rectangles. Or use a design of your own creation (look at old wine labels for inspiration). Fill in the lettering with brown paint. Allow paint to dry before continuing.

**3.** With **Right** sides together, sew the side pieces along the long edges using a ½" (1.3 cm) seam allowance. Press the seams open.

**4.** With **Right** sides together, sew the two tab pieces together along the long edges using a ¼" (6 mm) seam allowance. Turn **Right** side out and press. Topstitch close to the sewn edges. Cut the strip into four 4" (10 cm)-long pieces.

**5.** Center two tabs along the top edge of the bag on each side and baste in place. Fold the strips on each side over the bag handles and baste in place.

**6.** With **Right** sides together, sew the short ends of the facing piece together using a ½" (1.3 cm) seam allowance. Press the seam open. Press one edge under ½" (1.3 cm). With the **Right** sides together, sew the unpressed edge of the facing to the bag around the top edge, enclosing the tabs. Flip the facing to the inside of the bag and topstitch the pressed edge.

**7.** Turn bag **Right** side out. On the **Right** side of the bag, topstitch four pleats, 1¾" (4.5 cm) from the side seams, through the facing. Pleats should be 1½" (3.8 cm) long.

**8.** Turn bag inside out. With **Right** sides together, sew the bag to the bottom piece using a ½" (1.3 cm) seam allowance. Clip the seam allowance of the bag to fit around the corners. Turn bag **Right** side out again.

# ROLL-OUT PLACEMATS

*These simple placemats serve a picnic well—they have a pocket for utensils and a built-in napkin holder. Sewn out of old ticking, these placemats will last for years and become a family favorite. Roll up your placemats with flatware and a napkin inside and hand one out to each guest. All that's left to do is fill a plate with your favorite picnic food and enjoy the afternoon outdoors!*

## MATERIALS (FOR ONE PLACEMAT)

⅔ YARD (45" WIDE) (60 CM, 114 CM WIDE) RED TICKING

SCISSORS

IRON

SEWING MACHINE

## DIRECTIONS

**1.** Out of the red ticking, cut two rectangles, 21" (53 cm) wide by 15" (38 cm) long. For the pocket, cut one 6½"-by-5" (17 x 13 cm) rectangle on the bias. For the napkin tab and ties, cut a strip 1½" (3.8 cm) wide by 45" (114 cm) long.

**2.** Press both long edges of the strip under ¼" (6 mm). Fold the strip in half, bringing the pressed edges together with the **Right** side facing out, and topstitch the pressed edges together. Cut a 4" (10.2 cm)-long piece off one end of the strip for the napkin tab, and cut the remaining strip in half to make two ties.

**3.** Press under the ends of the napkin tab ½" (1.3 cm) and topstitch to the center of the left-hand side of one placemat piece. Center the ties along the left-hand edge, raw edges even with the placemat edge. Baste in place.

**4.** To make the pocket, turn under one short edge of the pocket piece ¼" (6 mm) and press. Turn under and press again ½" (1.3 cm) and topstitch the pressed edge. Turn under and press the remaining three edges ½" (1.3 cm) and

topstitch the pocket to the right-hand side of the placemat, leaving the top edge open.

**5.** With **Right** sides together, sew the two placemat pieces together using a ½" (1.3 cm) seam allowance around all sides, but leaving a 5" (12.7 cm) opening for turning inside out. Take care not to catch the ties in any of your seams. Turn **Right** side out and press. Topstitch around all the edges close to the finished edge and then again ½" from the finished edge.

# DINNER IN THE KITCHEN

*My father-in-law, Leandro Zabala, was a great Basque chef.*

---

LEANDRO LEARNED TO COOK AT AGE FOURTEEN WHILE LIVING IN A SEMINARY WITH THE JESUITS. HE WAS TAUGHT, FROM AN EARLY AGE, TWO KITCHEN RULES: FOOD MUST COME FROM A QUALITY SOURCE, AND FOOD MUST BE PREPARED SIMPLY. HE WOULD CONSTANTLY CALL ONE OF US OUT TO THE KITCHEN WHILE HE WAS COOKING TO SHOW US HOW FRESH SOMETHING WAS, HOW TO COOK WITH NO FUSS, AND, ALWAYS, HOW TO USE THE SCRAPS. ALTHOUGH LEN PREPARED A GRAND FEAST FOR US WHENEVER WE WERE TOGETHER, FOR HIMSELF HE PREFERRED A GOOD CUT OF MEAT, A FEW POTATOES, AND A SIDE OF VEGETABLES. NOTHING FANCY—JUST GOOD INGREDIENTS. ❋ LEN'S KITCHEN WAS SET UP LIKE A CHEF'S KITCHEN—APRON ALWAYS READY AT HAND, KNIVES SHARPENED AND IN THEIR OWN DRAWER, COPPER POTS SHINED AND READY TO USE, AND A BASKET FULL OF FRESH PRODUCE, MEAT, AND FISH READY TO BE CHOPPED, MIXED, SAUTÉED, AND SERVED. WHEN HE FINALLY DID SIT DOWN TO EAT, WITH A BOTTLE OF GOOD RIOJA NEXT TO HIM, HE ENJOYED THE MEAL AS MUCH AS, IF NOT MORE THAN, THE REST OF US. ❋ TO HONOR LEN, WE PREPARE A CHEF'S DINNER IN THE KITCHEN, COMPLETE WITH STEAK AND FRENCH FRIES—OR WHAT THE FRENCH HAVE PERFECTED, *STEAK FRITES.* 🐚

MENU

Steak with
Horseradish

Pomme frites

Asparagus

# A SIMPLE KITCHEN

Setting up a working kitchen doesn't have to be a huge investment. Start with the basics and slowly add pieces as needed. We have a knife drawer with a few well-sharpened knives that we've collected throughout the years. Five knives are all you need — a serrated blade, a paring knife, a 4" (10 cm) and an 8" (20 cm) blade, and a chef's knife for chopping.

Good, heavy-duty pots and pans in at least five sizes will get you through any meal: a 6" (15 cm) skillet, 10" (25 cm) skillet, 1-quart (0.9 liter) and 3-quart (2.8 liter) saucepans with lids, and a 4-gallon (15 liter) stockpot with lid. Look for stainless steel or enameled cast-iron pots and pans, as these will stand the test of time. I also enjoy cooking in our copper pans, as they distribute heat evenly.

My favorite piece in the kitchen is our cutting board, an old French butcher's board that shows years and years of use. Wash your cutting board with soap and water and let it dry thoroughly. Every once in a while give it a quick oiling with a mineral or olive oil to keep the wood looking fresh.

stem stitch

Tablier de Coq

# REDWORK ROOSTER APRON

*Ever since the French Revolution, the rooster has been the national emblem of France. We've interpreted this national symbol in our redwork rooster embroidery design. Try sewing this pattern onto an old hemp or linen tea towel, then fashion some ribbon or twill tape onto the sides for the ties. Made with long enough ties, this apron will be sure to fit anyone who takes their turn in the kitchen.*

## MATERIALS

LARGE WHITE DISH TOWEL

PENCIL

SEWING MACHINE

2 YARDS (½" WIDE) (1.8 METERS, 1.3 CM WIDE) WHITE COTTON TWILL TAPE

¼ YARD (45" WIDE) (23 CM, 114 CM WIDE) WHITE COTTON OR A SECOND DISH TOWEL

TRANSFER PAPER

RED EMBROIDERY FLOSS

EMBROIDERY NEEDLE

IRON

## DIRECTIONS

**1.** To make the apron: First, mark the center of the dish towel along one of the long edges. Measure your waist and then divide the number by 4. Mark on either side of the center by that number. For instance, if you have a 28" (71 cm) waist, you would make your side marks 7" (18 cm) from the center mark. Sew two ½" (1.3 cm) pleats at the side marks.

**2.** Mark the center of your twill tape and match with the center mark on the towel. Topstitch the twill tape to the towel with two rows of stitching, one close to one edge.

**3.** To make the pocket: On the white cotton or another dish towel, transfer the rooster design provided at the back of this book (see page 151). Embroider the entire design using a stem stitch. Cut out a 7" (18 cm) square with the rooster design in the center.

**4.** Press under the top edge of the square ¼" (6 mm). Press again ½" (1.3 cm) and topstitch the edge. Press under all other sides ½" (1.3 cm) and position the pocket where you like it best on the apron. Topstitch in place around three sides, leaving the top unsewn.

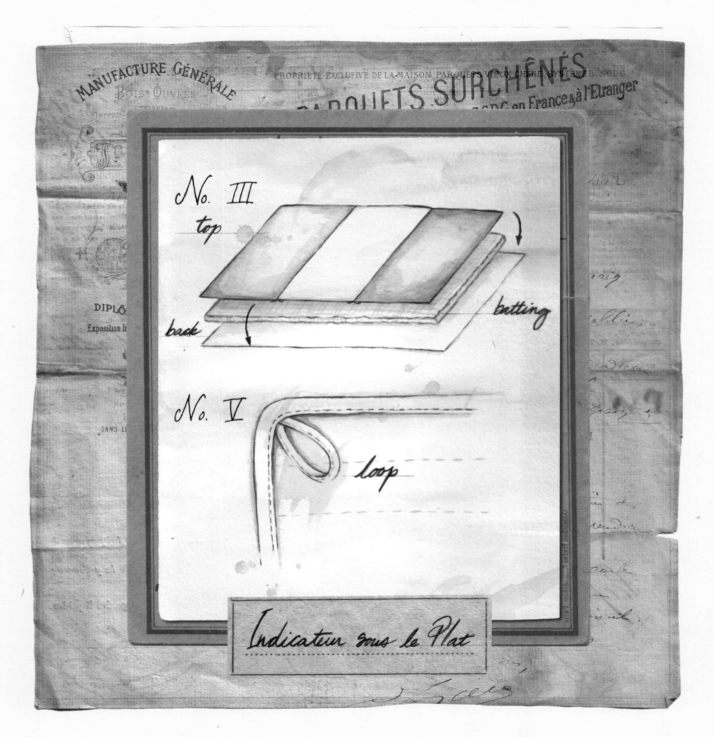

# FLAG TRIVET

*Use this simple trivet to protect your table from hot pots or as an oven mitt to carry food to the table. We designed this trivet with our French friends in mind, but you could of course use any flag's colors. Be sure to use fabric that can stand the heat—felt and flannel work well. When not in use on your table, hang from a small hook in the kitchen.*

## MATERIALS

¼ YARD (45" WIDE) (23 CM, 114 CM WIDE) BLUE FLANNEL

¼ YARD (45" WIDE) (23 CM, 114 CM WIDE) RED FLANNEL

¼ YARD (45" WIDE) (23 CM, 114 CM WIDE) WHITE FLANNEL

¼ YARD (45" WIDE) (23 CM, 114 CM WIDE) COTTON BATTING

SCISSORS

SEWING MACHINE

IRON

TAILOR'S CHALK

1 ¼ YARDS (½" WIDE) (114 CM, 1.3 CM WIDE) WHITE DOUBLE-FOLD BIAS TAPE

## DIRECTIONS

**1.** Out of the blue, red, and white flannel, cut a rectangle 4½" by 8" (11 x 20 cm). Out of the white flannel and the cotton batting, cut a rectangle 8" by 12" (20 x 30 cm). You may want to cut several layers of the batting depending on the thickness. You want the total thickness to be about ⅜".

**2.** Make the top by sewing the three small rectangles together along the 8" (20 cm) long sides, using a ½" (1.3 cm) seam allowance. Make sure the white piece is in the middle. Press the seams open.

**3.** Assemble the trivet with the large white flannel piece on the bottom, then the batting, then the top, **Right** side facing up. Baste all the layers together. Mark the quilting lines

1" (2.5 cm) apart with tailor's chalk, with the lines drawn vertically on the "flag." Quilt all the layers together by machine, starting in the center and working outward to each side. Trim any excess batting around the edges. Trim corner points into a small curve.

**4.** Make a loop of bias tape by topstitching a 4" (10 cm) piece and folding into a 2" (5 cm) loop, and baste the loop to one corner on the white side of the quilted piece.

**5.** Cover the raw edges of the trivet with the folded bias and topstitch in place. The bias should cover the raw ends of the loop made in step 4. Fold the raw ends of the bias inside before stitching.

# MENU BOARD

*Start out your dinner in the kitchen by passing around a menu board to let each of your guests know what specialties you have prepared for the meal. A small chalkboard from the craft shop, a decorative wooden header, and some paint make up this simple project. For an old bistro look, sand down the edges of the board after painting, and your guests will feel as if they are in* la cuisine de la maison.

## MATERIALS

SMALL CHALKBOARD IN WOODEN FRAME

UNPAINTED WOOD TRIM (SOLD IN CRAFT AND MODEL STORES)

WOOD GLUE

ACRYLIC PAINT

CARDSTOCK

X-ACTO KNIFE

PAINTER'S TAPE

GOLD ACRYLIC PAINT OR MARKER

SMALL PAINTBRUSH

## DIRECTIONS

**1.** Attach the trim to the chalkboard using wood glue. Once the glue is dry, paint the chalkboard frame and trim with paint. To achieve a vintage look, rub paint off of the raised areas and edges with a cloth while it is still slightly wet.

**2.** Copy the "menu" design provided at the back of the book (see page 161) onto the cardstock. Using an X-Acto knife and drawing the blade away from you, carefully cut out the letters to make a stencil. Tape the stencil onto the chalkboard frame and fill in the letters with gold paint. Or, using a gold marker, hand-write "menu" or anything you wish as the board's heading.

**3.** Display on a small easel or hang on the wall.

# MOULES FRITES FÊTE

*I am the first to admit that I am not a huge shellfish eater — but smother mussels with white wine, butter, garlic, and shallots, and they're hard to resist.*

SOMETHING ABOUT THE TASTY BROTH SURROUNDING THE SHELLS—TURNING IT INTO A SOUP—WINS ME OVER EVERY TIME. ❄ MUSSELS CANNOT BE SERVED ALL YEAR ROUND—I'VE LEARNED THEY ARE ONLY AVAILABLE FRESH IN THE MONTHS THAT CONTAIN THE LETTER "R." SO COME SEPTEMBER, START LOOKING OUT FOR THESE SHINY, BLACK PINCHER-TYPE SHELLS, WHICH ARE BEST SERVED IN A BOILING BROTH WITH A SIDE OF FRIES AND A FRESH BAGUETTE. IT ALL SOUNDS RATHER DECADENT, SO THINK OF *MOULES FRITES* AS A TREAT RATHER THAN A STAPLE. THEY GET MESSY, SO SERVE WITH PLENTY OF NAPKINS, OR EVEN HOMEMADE TEA TOWEL APRONS (SEE PAGE 93) TO KEEP YOUR GUESTS SPLATTER FREE. ✺

# APRON ANYONE?

*When serving a potentially messy seafood meal,
consider offering your guests an apron to keep their
clothes free of broth or sauce.*

To make a handful of aprons before your
guests arrive, pull out extra tea towels and tack
on ribbon to the top sides of each towel.

**LEAVE THE RIBBON LENGTHS
EXTRA LONG SO THAT THEY CAN FIT AROUND
ANYONE'S WAIST.**

When the aprons start looking a little
worse for wear after many meals, I throw them
into a boiling pot of dye and give
them a new color—this works wonders on
hiding old stains.

A. BON
BOUCHER, CHARCUTIER
LA TESTE (Gir.)

# NAUTICAL BUCKETS

*To set the mood for your moules frites night, look for galvanized buckets and paint them with the names of classic old French fishing ports—or your favorite seaside towns. Use smaller tins to make favors; paint guests' names onto them and fill with parsley plants or line with brown paper to hold the frites.*

## MATERIALS

FOOD-SAFE METAL BUCKETS

ENAMEL PAINT IN BLUE AND OFF-WHITE
(NONTOXIC, AIR-DRYING FINISH RATHER THAN BAKE-ON)

SPONGE BRUSHES

PAINTER'S TAPE

HEAVY CARDSTOCK

X-ACTO KNIFE

SMALL PAINTBRUSH

## DIRECTIONS

**1.** Using a sponge brush, paint the outside of your buckets off-white with a blue stripe in the middle. Use painter's tape to get a clean paint line.

**2.** Copy the seaside French names provided on page 147. Using an X-Acto knife and drawing the blade away from you, carefully cut out the letters to make a stencil. Save any letters that have interior lines, such as A, B, O, and R, and cut out the interior spaces.

**3.** Tape the stencil onto your bucket, centering the lettering on the blue stripe. If your bucket has slanted sides, you may need to cut slits in the upper edge of the stencil so it hugs the curve well. Using a small paintbrush, fill in the letters with off-white paint. Allow the paint to dry a bit before removing the stencil.

**4.** Once the letters are completely dry, reapply any letters that need interior lines painted. Fill in the interior spaces with blue paint.

**5.** Paint the frites cups in the same manner, omitting the lettering.

# STAMPED LINENS

*Linoleum block–stamped linens are the perfect casual cloth to set your table with. Use the nautical-inspired stencils we've designed (see page 162) or create your own shapes. In lieu of a guestbook, consider letting guests stamp their names onto the tablecloth with alphabet stamps. Be sure to use fabric paint so that your designs will last for years and years to come.*

## MATERIALS

TRANSFER PAPER

LINOLEUM BLOCKS

LINOLEUM CARVING TOOLS

LINEN TABLECLOTH AND/OR NAPKINS
(BUY EXTRA IN CASE OF MISTAKES)

PENCIL

SCRAP CARDBOARD OR FOAM CORE

NAVY BLUE FABRIC PAINT OR INK

SMALL TRAY

SMALL INK ROLLER

## DIRECTIONS

**1.** Copy the stamp designs provided in the back of the book (see page 162) by photocopying them or scanning and printing them. Using transfer paper, trace the designs onto linoleum blocks. Before carving, mark the areas you will cut away (the interior lines and the space around the design). Carve out with linoleum tools.

**2.** Alternatively, you can make rubber stamps from the designs, use the designs as stencils, or trace the designs directly onto your linens and paint them. Or create your own designs and stamp those!

**3.** Mark the areas on your linens that you plan to stamp with a light pencil. To make a tablecloth border, divide each edge

evenly and make all your stamp marks the same distance from the finished edge.

**4.** Place cardboard or foam core under the linens for a slightly cushioned yet firm surface to stamp on.

**5.** Pour your paint or ink into a small tray. Using the roller, cover your stamp with paint. Position the stamp and press firmly onto the fabric. You'll need to work fairly quickly, as you don't want the paint to dry on the stamp before you transfer it to the fabric.

**6.** Let the stamped linens dry completely before moving them. Launder according to the directions on your paint or ink.

# SHELL VOTIVES

*To add a bit of light to your moules frites night, try pouring candle wax into shells that you have collected. We used oyster shells we found on the shore in Seabeck, but you can use scallop shells just as easily. The deeper the shell, the longer the votives will burn. The shells can be recycled and used over and over again—just clean them out and repour new wax.*

## MATERIALS

ASSORTED SHELLS

BLEACH

SCRUB BRUSH

CANDLE WAX

DOUBLE BOILER

KITCHEN THERMOMETER

RICE OR SAND (OPTIONAL)

PREMADE CANDLE WICKS

## DIRECTIONS

**1.** Start by thoroughly cleaning the shells, using warm water mixed with a few drops of bleach and a stiff scrub brush. Let the shells dry completely—at least twenty-four hours.

**2.** Melt the wax in a double boiler over medium heat, following the directions on the package. Use a thermometer to make sure you do not overheat the wax.

**3.** While the wax is melting, set up your shells. If the shells won't sit up straight on their own, rest them in a dish filled with rice or sand. Place a wick in the deepest part of each shell.

**4.** Carefully pour the wax into each shell, taking care not to move the wick. Allow the candles to cool according to the wax package directions.

**5.** Before lighting the candles, trim the wicks to about ¼" (6 mm).

# POOLSIDE GRILL DINNER

*When we moved back to California from New York, I knew one thing:*
*I wanted a home with a pool.*

———— ✦ ————

SINCE I GREW UP ON THE WEST COAST WITH A VIEW OF THE OCEAN FROM OUR KITCHEN WINDOW, I WANTED TO SEE WATER—EVEN IF IT WAS ONLY IN MY BACKYARD. THE OLD SPANISH HOUSE WE FOUND IN LOS FELIZ HAS A MAJESTIC POOL, ONE THAT HAD BEEN BUILT BACK IN THE 1950S WHEN POOLS COULD BE DEEP AND BIG. ✳ EVEN IF YOU DON'T HAVE A POOL, GRILLING ON A BARBECUE MAKES GATHERINGS DURING THE WARM SUMMER MONTHS A REAL TREAT. YOU CAN COME UP WITH DIFFERENT COMBINATIONS OF WHAT CAN BE GRILLED ON A STICK BEFORE FRIENDS ARRIVE, OR EVERYONE CAN MAKE THEIR OWN CUSTOM KEBABS. SET UP A TABLE WITH A VARIETY OF MEATS, SEAFOOD, AND VEGETABLES AND HAVE A HANDFUL OF WOODEN SKEWERS THAT HAVE BEEN SOAKED OVERNIGHT IN WATER (TO AVOID BURNING ON THE GRILL). ❦

# BUFFET IDEAS

Letting people serve themselves is the simplest way to throw a party. Preplanning the food table as well as the drinks bar makes for an event where you can actually sit down and enjoy your guests. After deciding on your menu, choose your serving platters and tools. Set up your buffet table starting with plates, utensils, and napkins, then lay out the food in the order you would like to serve it—if you are setting up a salad bar, start with the salad first and then set up all of your mixings, putting the dressing and salt and pepper at the end.

For a drinks bar, set out glasses in a few different sizes, a bucket of ice, and a selection of drinks. Have some bottles of wine or champagne open and be sure to offer a pitcher of water with lemon slices. Cutting up small garnishes lets friends have fun with their drinks—a slice of orange is perfect for a glass of Lillet, and mint is nice with lemonade.

# FABRIC BANNERS

*For a festive night, try making our Matisse-inspired banners to hang around the outdoor area—although simple to make, they add a bit of elegance to an old pool, patio, or deck. We used a teal-dyed hemp sheet with white linen cutouts for a fresh look. Think about using any sort of canvas or even burlap and then design a cutout for the center. I grew up with fabric banners that were recycled year after year for every sort of celebration. "Erin go Bragh" on shamrock-printed fabric was my favorite.*

## MATERIALS (FOR ONE BANNER)

1 YARD (91 CM) TURQUOISE HEMP OR LINEN

SCISSORS

SEWING MACHINE

IRON

½ YARD NO-SEW IRON-ON ADHESIVE
(THE KIND WITH A PAPER BACKING)

½ YARD WHITE HEMP OR LINEN

TRANSFER PAPER

## DIRECTIONS

**1.** From the turquoise hemp, cut a rectangle 32" long by 25" (81 x 63 cm) wide. Hem the long sides and one short side by turning under ½" (1.3 cm), pressing, and then turning under ½" (1.3 cm) again and topstitching. Make a pocket in the top by turning under ½" (1.3 cm), pressing, and then turning under 1" (2.5 cm) and topstitching, leaving the sides open.

**2.** Iron the adhesive to the white linen, paper side facing up. Allow fabric to cool. Transfer the designs provided in the back of the book for the four border shapes (see pages 152 to 155) and Matisse shapes (see pages 156 to 160) to the paper side of the adhesive. Cut out the appliqués. Do not add a seam allowance.

**3.** Working on one appliqué at a time, peel the paper backing off and position on the banner. Iron the appliqué to the banner following the directions on the adhesive package.

**4.** If you use a "no-sew" adhesive, your banner is ready to hang. However, if you want a different look, you can use adhesive that is meant to be sewn and topstitch around the edges of the appliqués after ironing them down.

# LUMINARIES

*For a soft poolside glow when the sun begins to set, light a bunch of luminaries, or paper bag lanterns. Our lights are made the old-fashioned way, using white paper bags with a candle sitting on sand in the bottom. For a colorful look, cut out shapes from tissue paper and layer one color on top of another. This is a great kids craft—just let them tear the tissue paper into scraps and then layer onto the paper bag with glue and a brush.*

## MATERIALS (FOR ONE LUMINARY)

TISSUE PAPER IN ASSORTED COLORS

SCISSORS

WHITE PAPER LUNCH BAG

PIECE OF CARDBOARD OR THIN PLASTIC THE SAME SIZE AS YOUR BAG

WHITE GLUE

PAINTBRUSH

SAND

VOTIVE CANDLE AND GLASS HOLDER

## DIRECTIONS

**1.** Using the patterns provided in the back of the book (see pages 156 to 160), cut two of the Matisse-inspired shapes out of tissue paper. Cut or tear other shapes and strips out of different-colored tissue paper.

**2.** Slip the cardboard or plastic inside the bag so that you don't glue the bag shut as you work on it.

**3.** Using a mixture of equal parts white glue and water, glue the paper shapes to the bag. Paint a thin layer of glue onto the bag, apply the tissue paper, and then seal with another layer of glue. Once the tissue paper is wet, you will have very little time to move it around, so place your shapes carefully.

**4.** Wait until one side of the bag is totally dry before working on the second side.

**5.** When displaying your luminaries, fill the bag with a couple inches of sand so that it won't blow over. Rest the votive holder in the sand. If the bag does tip over, the sand should extinguish the flame. However, you should not leave luminaries unattended or place them near anything that can catch fire.

# EMBROIDERED COCKTAIL NAPKINS

*The cocktail napkin became a necessity when cocktail soirées included small snacks. Offer your guests a small hand-stitched cocktail napkin—the perfect size for a little bite to eat and an early-evening cocktail. In keeping with our outdoor French flavor, we hand-stitched ours with Matisse-inspired shapes for a timeless look.*

## MATERIALS

WHITE LINEN COCKTAIL NAPKINS, ABOUT 5" BY 7" (12 × 17 CM)

TRANSFER PAPER

EMBROIDERY FLOSS IN SHADES OF TURQUOISE

EMBROIDERY NEEDLE

## DIRECTIONS

**1.** Make or buy white linen cocktail napkins.

**2.** Using the design provided in the back of the book (see page 161), transfer the Matisse shape to a corner of each napkin.

**3.** Outline and fill the shape using a chain stitch.

**4.** Finish the edge of the napkin (using a different color) with a buttonhole stitch. A buttonhole stitch is worked in the same way as a blanket stitch; the stitches are just closer together.

# MIDSUMMER'S EVE

*The long days and hot nights of summer are perfect for setting up
an outdoor table and inviting your
friends to gather round to celebrate the summer solstice.*

———————

MIDSUMMER WAS ONCE THOUGHT TO BE A MAGICAL TIME, WHEN FAIRIES AND ANIMALS APPEARED AND DANCED TOGETHER. PEOPLE WORE GARLANDS OF HERBS AND FLOWERS TO BLESS THEMSELVES FOR THE COMING YEAR. ❋ SETTING UP SMALL OUTDOOR TABLES IN THE GARDEN, COVERED WITH OLD LINEN AND HEMP, CREATES AN ETHEREAL ATMOSPHERE. FRESH, LOCAL FOOD SUCH AS GRILLED CHICKEN SERVED WITH WILD MUSHROOM SALAD, ARUGULA, AND SLICED GRILLED POTATOES MAKES A MEAL FIT FOR VISITING RABBITS. FINISH THE DINNER WITH A MAJESTIC DESSERT—SOMETHING OVER THE TOP THAT WILL KEEP EVERYONE IN A FESTIVE MOOD LONG AFTER THE SUN HAS SET. ❧

# A FAMILY AFFAIR

*Having friends and family gather means planning
different activities for different ages.*

Think about how everyone can be involved with
the organizing and entertaining. Supplying masks
or dress-up materials is always a big hit—as is pro-
viding musical instruments for people to strum a
few chords. A game of cards or checkers is the perfect after-dinner entertainment for all ages. Stick to
a simple menu and let people serve themselves—so
everyone can find something they enjoy eating.
Throughout the years, my parents have always
combined all ages when entertaining, which I think
taught us to engage with the adults at an early age.

# ORGANZA CHAIR COVER

*A simple chair cover made with elegant fabric turns an ordinary French garden chair into a regal seat. We sewed our covers out of embroidered cotton organza—it is crisp enough to not be too drapey on the chair. If you don't have time to sew covers for your chairs, wrap a lightweight fabric around each chair, letting it drape a little onto the ground. Finish by placing a 3" (7.6 cm)-wide ribbon around the back of the seat and tying a bow in the back of the chair, which adds a pretty skirt around the legs.*

## MATERIALS (FOR ONE CHAIR)

PAPER FOR PATTERN

PENCIL

APPROX. 1 ½ YARDS (60" WIDE) (1.4 METERS, 1.5 METERS WIDE) COTTON ORGANZA

SCISSORS

IRON

SEWING MACHINE

## DIRECTIONS

**1.** Measure the chair to be covered, and on your pattern paper draw pieces for the seat, the seat back, the chair back, the skirt front, and the skirt sides. On each skirt piece, add 3" (7.6 cm) to the total width measurement (for pleats). Add a ½" (1.3 cm) seam allowance to all sides of your pattern pieces. If you want the skirt to skim the floor, add ½" (1.3 cm) to the bottom edge of the skirt pieces; if you want it to drape on the floor, add 1½" (3.9 cm). The chair back and seat back pieces should fit loosely, as they will be cinched with the ties when finished.

**2.** Cut one seat, one seat back, one chair back, one skirt front, and two skirt sides from the cotton organza. Cut two strips 28" long by 2½" (71 x 6 cm) wide for the ties.

**3.** Make the ties by folding each one in half lengthwise

and sewing the long edge and one short end using a ¼" seam allowance. Turn **Right** side out and press.

**4.** Sew the three skirt pieces together at the side seams using a ½" (1.3 cm) seam allowance. Finish the side edges and bottom edge by turning under ¼" (6 mm) twice and topstitching.

**5.** Sew the skirt to three sides of the seat, making ½" (1.3 cm) pleats at each corner. Sew the bottom of the seat back to the fourth side of the seat.

**6.** Sew the chair back to the seat back, sandwiching one tie on each side of the seat back. Finish the bottom and open sides of the chair back by turning under ¼" (6 mm) twice and topstitching.

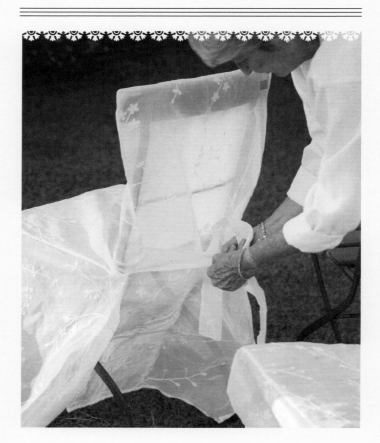

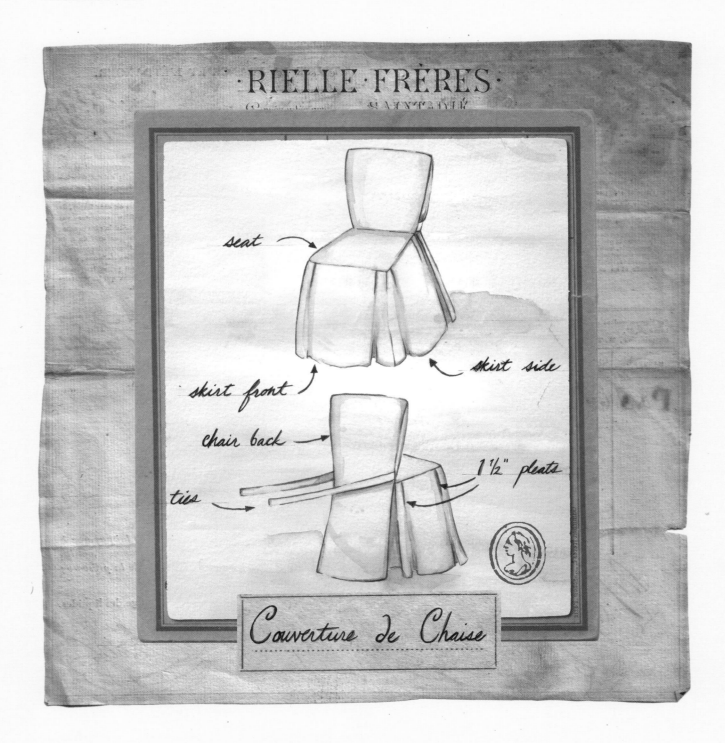

RIELLE·FRÈRES·

seat

skirt side

skirt front

chair back

1 ½" pleats

ties

Couverture de Chaise

# FAUX BOIS VOTIVES

*A fantasy evening in the garden needs creative lighting. With a simple
stencil and a bit of paint, you can paint a faux bois pattern on glass
votives. Clean out any old glass jars for this project—old jam jars
are a good size for most candles—or look for inexpensive votives
at your craft store. Use the pattern we provide (see page 149) for a
wood-grain look or make a stencil out of clear adhesive paper.*

## MATERIALS

GLASS VOTIVE HOLDERS, ABOUT 3" IN DIAMETER

SCISSORS

MASKING TAPE

OFF-WHITE GLASS OR CERAMIC PAINT
(AIR DRYING RATHER THAN BAKE-ON FINISH)

SMALL PAINTBRUSH

FLOATING VOTIVE CANDLES

## DIRECTIONS

**1.** Photocopy the wood-grain design provided in the back of
the book (see page 149), or scan it and print out.

**2.** Trim the copy so it fits inside the votive holder. Tape the
copy inside the glass with the printed side facing out.

**3.** With a small paintbrush, copy the wood-grain pattern onto
the outside of the glass using the off-white glass paint. Don't
worry about copying the pattern exactly—the more unique
it is, the better. Work in sections, allowing each section to dry
before moving on.

**4.** When the paint is dry, remove the paper from the glass.
Fill the glass about half full with water and float a votive
candle inside. Wash according to the directions on your
glass paint.

# VENETIAN ANIMAL MASK

*Visiting rabbits can arrive in their fine whites and a new mask made to look old with a little magic. Embellish ordinary masks with a bit of brown paper, a brush of paint, and a sparkle of mica to bring out the whimsical mood of the night. You can also add a 12" (30 cm) wooden dowel to the chin of each mask to allow guests to disguise themselves when necessary.*

## MATERIALS

PLASTIC ANIMAL MASK (FOUND IN DRUGSTORES, COSTUME SHOPS, OR ONLINE)

BROWN CRAFT PAPER OR PLAIN BROWN PAPER BAGS

WHITE GLUE

WATERCOLOR PAINTS

PAINTBRUSHES

GLITTER OR MICA

SINGLE-HOLE PUNCH

GOLD ELASTIC

RIBBONS

## DIRECTIONS

1. If the mask already has elastic attached, remove it.

2. Tear the brown paper into small strips of varying lengths but all about ½" (1.3 cm) wide. In a small bowl, make a mixture of equal parts white glue and water.

3. Soak a paper strip in the glue until slightly soft, then apply to the mask. While the strip is still soft and pliable, mold it with your fingers to the shape of the mask, getting into any creases or folds. Keep applying strips in this manner until the mask is completely covered. Make sure to cover the edges and eye or mouth hole edges as well, wrapping the strip around to the inside. (This is a messy process but perfect for kids to help with!)

4. After letting the first layer of paper dry completely, apply another layer. Keep building up layers until you are happy with the finish.

5. Using watercolor paints, paint details on the mask such as fur, whiskers, and a nose. Leaving the brown paper visible on much of the mask adds to the vintage look. Apply glitter where desired by painting on white glue and sprinkling with glitter.

6. Punch holes into the sides of the mask for attaching elastic and ribbon. Cut the gold elastic so it fits snugly and tie with a double knot on each side. Tie on ribbons in varying colors and lengths.

# HARVEST DINNER

*I have an old table that my grandmother used as her dining room table.*

———————— ❖ ————————

WHENEVER IT WAS THRASHER SEASON—THE SEASON WHEN THE FIELDS WERE HARVESTED—SHE WOULD PULL OUT THE LEAVES AND TURN THE SMALL, HUMBLE TABLE INTO ONE THAT COULD SEAT SIXTEEN PEOPLE. I LIKE TO IMAGINE THESE THRASHERS CAME INTO A VERY SIMPLE ROOM WHEREIN THE TABLE HAD BEEN SET IN AN ELEGANT BUT RUSTIC SORT OF WAY, ADORNED WITH RICHES FROM HER GARDEN. ❋ I DON'T KNOW ANY THRASHERS, BUT I DO ENJOY SERVING A MEAL AROUND MY GRANDMOTHER'S WELL-WORN TABLE. I PULL OUT ALL OF MY EARLY-AMERICAN SERVING PIECES—OLD BREAD DOUGH BOWLS FOR A MIXED SALAD, EARTHENWARE CASSOULET POTS, BLACK CAST-IRON PANS, AND WATER GOBLETS FOR WINE. SERVING UP FORAGED FOOD LIKE SNAILS AND MUSHROOMS CAN ADD A BIT OF THE BIZARRE TO YOUR TABLE. ❧

# VESSELS AND VASES

*Arranging flowers and greenery in your home can add so much to a modest gathering. Look for all sorts of containers that can be used to hold water and a handful of leaves, flowers, or sprigs. Old pitchers, cans, buckets, jam jars, and Crock-Pots can all become vessels to hold a fresh arrangement.*

When displaying natural elements, always start with clean water and cut your stems at an angle. Woody stems can be crushed with a small hammer. Use an old glass frog or a florist sponge to make your arrangement hold its place—or put a bushel of hand-picked flowers into your vase for a fresh, natural display. Instead of buying flowers, look for what's growing right outside your home. Lavender, rosemary, ivy? Bringing the garden into the house will make you want to tend a garden.

# VEGETABLE CENTERPIECE

*Something over the top and completely fun became our centerpiece for this rustic dinner. While visiting our local farmers' market in Hollywood, we looked for unusually shaped and colored root vegetables. We picked up seasonal herbs and lettuces and put our friend Jody to work. Built in a basket, the arrangement could be made smaller using a bowl or even a tureen. For the filling, look in your own garden first and then build upon what you have.*

## MATERIALS

LARGE BOWL OR BASKET

FLORIST'S FOAM

KITCHEN SCISSORS OR SHARP KNIVES

WOODEN SKEWERS AND TOOTHPICKS

ASSORTED VEGETABLES

## DIRECTIONS

**1.** Cut a piece of foam a few inches smaller than the inside of your container. Cut additional foam in graduated sizes, stacking the pieces until you reach the desired height and the foam has a roughly conical shape. Use skewers to hold the layers together.

**2.** Start the first row of vegetables at the bottom of the cone. It is best to put the heaviest items at the bottom, such as potatoes or beets. Stick a toothpick halfway into the vegetable, then stick it into the foam. Start the first row low enough into the bowl so that you can't see any foam underneath and the veggies fill the bowl.

**3.** Continue adding more vegetables in rows until you reach the top of the foam. Finish off the top with a crown of carrots, asparagus, or greens. Fill in any empty spaces with sprigs of herbs or parsley.

CHARDIN

kale

mushroom

squash

radish

eggplant

cauliflower

artichoke

turnip

Bouquet Végétal

MÉDAILLE DE 1re CLASSE
(LA PLUS HAUTE RÉCOMPENSE DÉCERNÉE AU GROUPE DU BOIS)

Exposition des ARTS DÉCORATIFS
PARIS, 1884

# BOTANICAL PLACEMATS

*These classic linen placemats are not only interesting to look at, but a whole set can comprise a botanical study series. Look for a collection of old drawings or images for variety—a set of insects could change the theme of the party. With the prints transferred onto linen with an iron, these placemats will withstand washing and hold up for years with a little extra care. Take care in only ironing the back side of the placemat, as the heat will melt the artwork otherwise.*

## MATERIALS

LINEN PLACEMATS

BLACK-AND-WHITE BOTANICAL PRINTS
(FOUND IN CLIP-ART BOOKS)

FABRIC TRANSFER PAPER FOR INKJET PRINTER
(AVAILABLE IN CRAFT STORES)

SCISSORS

IRON

## DIRECTIONS

**1.** Make or buy linen placemats, around 14" by 20" (36 x 51 cm).

**2.** Scan some botanical prints that you like and size them in a photoediting program to be about 10" (25.4 cm) tall. If the images contain words, reverse the image (the transfer will read the right way once it's ironed on). Print the images onto transfer paper made for ironing onto fabric. You can also take your images to a copy shop and have them made into transfers there.

**3.** Using sharp scissors, carefully cut out the transfers very close to the edge of the image. The transfer paper will change the look of the fabric slightly, so it's best to cut away as much as possible.

**4.** Iron the transfers onto your placemats, following the directions on the transfer paper package.

# DECOUPAGE VASES

*Recycled cans make the perfect vessels for these decoupage vases. Look for old images that you can cut out and paste onto a painted can. Guests will be happy to receive these gifts at the end of a meal.*

## MATERIALS

FULL-COLOR BOTANICAL PRINTS

X-ACTO KNIFE OR SMALL SCISSORS

BLACK PERMANENT MARKER

LARGE METAL CANS (WE USED 28-OZ. TOMATO CANS)

PLIERS OR TIN SNIPS

BLACK ACRYLIC PAINT

SPONGE BRUSHES

MOD PODGE OR OTHER DECOUPAGE MEDIUM

BONE FOLDER OR WOODEN SPOON

CLEAR ACRYLIC SEALANT

## DIRECTIONS

**1.** Make color copies of botanical prints. You can find images in clip-art books, calendars, or magazines. The images on seed packets also work well. Carefully cut out the images using an X-Acto knife or scissors so that no white background is visible. To avoid cutting out tiny interior spaces, fill them in with a black marker.

**2.** Empty and clean your cans. Use pliers or tin snips to get rid of any sharp edges around the opening.

**3.** Paint the exterior of the cans black with the acrylic paint. When the paint is completely dry, glue your botanical prints onto the can using Mod Podge or other decoupage medium. Use the bone folder or the handle of a wooden spoon to mold the prints into any ridges on the can.

**4.** Once the prints are dry, cover the entire can and prints with a layer of Mod Podge. Once dry, layer with acrylic sealant.

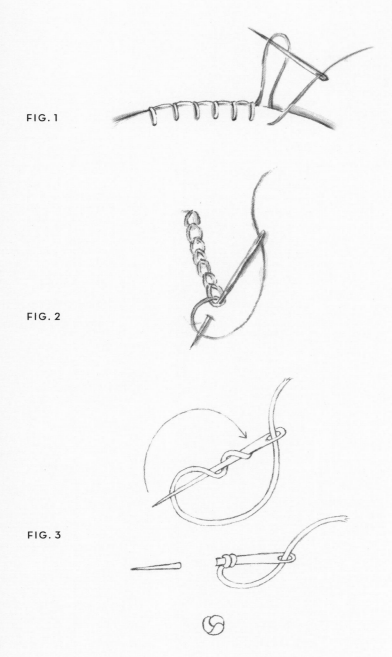

FIG. 1

FIG. 2

FIG. 3

# GENERAL TECHNIQUES

## BIAS

The bias of a fabric is the 45-degree angle from the top edge to the side edge. Bias-cut fabric is often used for edging and covering cord to make piping, because it has a certain amount of stretchiness to it. You can buy bias tape in a variety of colors and widths, or make your own by cutting strips on the bias and stitching them together.

## EMBROIDERY STITCHES

### BLANKET STITCH, FIG. 1

Bring your needle up through the fabric from underneath, about ¼" (6 mm) from the edge to be covered. Passing the needle under the thread coming from behind the work, take another stitch from underneath, and pull the stitch up to form a loop. Continue working in a straight line, from left to right.

### CHAIN STITCH, FIG. 2

Bring your needle out on the line of the design, and hold the thread to the left with a finger. Insert the needle again in the same place, taking a small stitch along the line of the design and keeping the looped thread under the point of the needle. Pull the thread through to form a small loop on the surface of the fabric.

### FRENCH KNOT, FIG. 3

Pull thread out from behind fabric at desired spot. Holding excess thread out of the way with your thumb, wind the thread around the needle several times. While still holding the excess, insert the needle back in the fabric, close to the starting point. Pull excess through, tightening the knot on the surface of the fabric.

## SATIN STITCH, FIG. 4

Cover the shape to be filled with a series of straight stitches placed very close together, varying the length of the stitches depending on the outline of the design. To achieve a raised satin stitch, outline the shape first using a split stitch. Then cover the outline stitching with satin stitches.

## SPLIT STITCH, FIG. 5

Start with a straight stitch on the line of your design. Bring your needle up through the fabric and pierce the straight stitch, "splitting" the threads. Continue working this way along the design from left to right.

## STEM STITCH, FIG. 6

Working from left to right, make small, slanting stitches along the line you wish to outline. The beginning of each stitch should always be to the left of the previous stitch.

## STRAIGHT STITCH, FIG. 7

Come up through the back of the fabric at the desired place and reinsert your needle back through the top of the fabric a little farther away from where you came out. Pull thread through.

## WHIPSTITCH, FIG. 8

To close a seam opening using a whip stitch, first make sure the seam allowances are turned inside the project. Working from left to right, bring your needle up through the lower edge of the seam opening from underneath the fabric. Make a small diagonal stitch to the right, catching the upper edge of the seam before you bring your needle back through the lower edge. Continue making small diagonal stitches until the opening is closed.

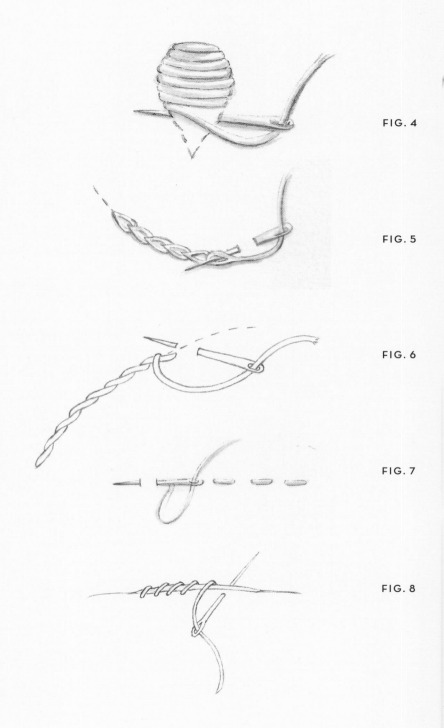

FIG. 4

FIG. 5

FIG. 6

FIG. 7

FIG. 8

## SEAM ALLOWANCE

Seam allowance is the extra fabric you need to make a seam. Seam allowance can be any size, but most projects in this book call for a ½" (1.3 cm) seam allowance. Seam allowance is usually hidden inside a garment or project, but you should still finish the edges of your seams somehow to prevent fraying. Common methods for finishing seams are pinking, zigzagging, and overcasting or serging. You can also cover the seam allowance with another fabric such as bias tape or twill tape. This is a good method for items that will be washed a lot, or when the seams will be visible.

## TOPSTITCHING

Topstitching is a line of stitching that is done on top of the fabric and will be visible, unlike a seam. Topstitching is often used for hems, can be used to strengthen a seam, or to make the seam allowance lie a certain way. Topstitching also adds a professional, finished look to many projects.

## TRANSFERS

There are many ways to transfer a design onto fabric, and experienced crafters use a variety of these techniques. My favorite method is to use a light box or window under the fabric. Make a photocopy of your design and tape the photocopy to the light box or a brightly lit window with masking tape. Place your fabric over the photocopy and, if necessary, tape the fabric in place. Then simply trace the design onto your fabric using a pencil or washable fabric marker. For transferring designs onto especially thick or dark fabrics, I use carbon transfer tracing paper, which is available at craft and fabric stores. Make a photocopy of your design, and place the carbon transfer paper between the photocopy and the fabric. Make sure to place the carbon side of the paper against your material. Trace your design, pressing firmly with a dull pencil, and the design will be transferred.

## TURNING CORNERS

Sewing a right angle is a basic skill you must have to make nice-looking corners on your projects. The secret to a sharp corner is simply to make sure your needle is in the down position, through your fabric, at the point where you want to turn. Lift the machine's presser foot, turn your fabric with the needle still in it, and put your presser foot back down. Now you can continue stitching in the new direction and you have made a perfect corner! When you are ready to turn your seam right side out, trim the seam allowance at the corner so it doesn't bunch up inside. Cut away the seam allowance at a 45-degree angle from the edges, but don't cut too close to your stitching or you may poke through when you turn it.

## ZIPPERS

There are many ways to sew a zipper into a seam, and all experienced sewers have their own favorite methods. Typically, the easiest method is to topstitch the zipper in place. Start by basting closed the opening in the seam where you want a zipper. Press the seam open. With the **Wrong** side of the seam facing up, and the **Right** side of the zipper facing down, hand-baste the zipper in place, making sure the zipper teeth are centered over the seam. Take out the basting in the fabric seam. Now you can topstitch on the **Right** side of the fabric, about ⅛" from the seam, all the way around your zipper. If you do not have a zipper foot on your machine, simply move the zipper pull up or down (while keeping your machine needle in the fabric) to get around it.

# PATTERN PIECES

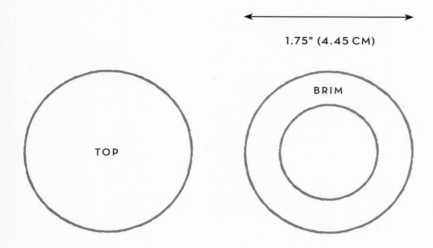

1.75" (4.45 CM)

BRIM

TOP

PATTERNS USED IN "EGG BERETS" ON PAGE 28. SHOWN AT 100%.

PATTERNS USED IN "EMBROIDERED JAM COVERS" ON PAGE 27. SHOWN AT 100%.

# ST. MALO
# SETE
# MARSEILLES
# CANCALE
# ST. MAXIME
# ANTIBES

PATTERNS USED IN "NAUTICAL BUCKETS" ON PAGE 94. INCREASE BY 118%.

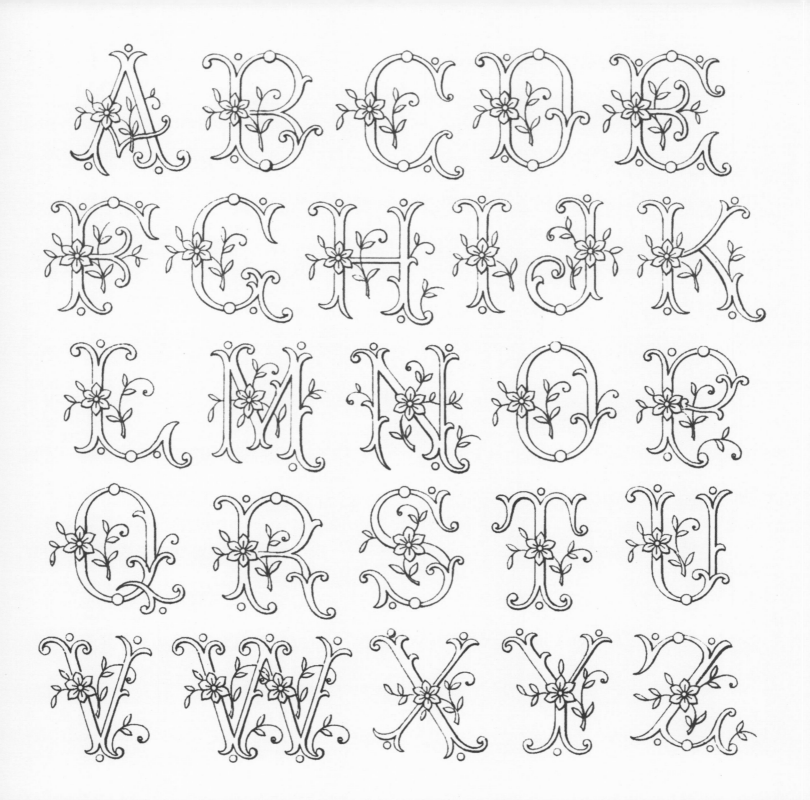

PATTERNS USED IN "MONOGRAMMED NAPKINS" ON PAGE 46. SHOWN AT 100%.

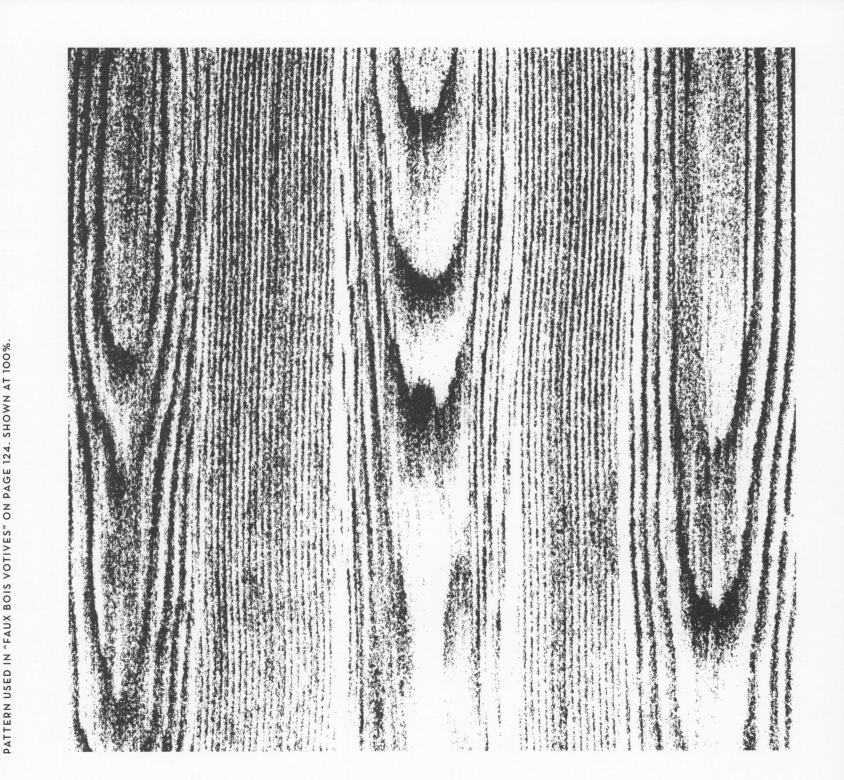

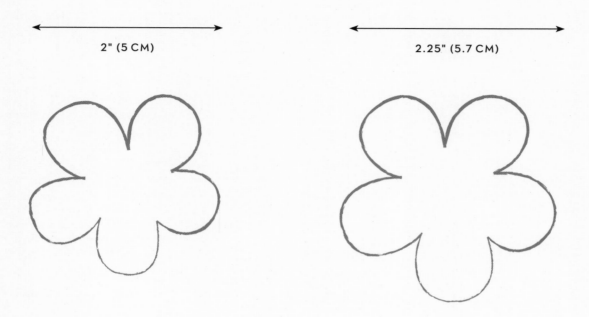

2" (5 CM)

2.25" (5.7 CM)

PATTERNS USED IN "FLORAL LANTERNS" ON PAGE 44. SHOWN AT 100%.

PATTERN USED IN "REDWORK ROOSTER APRON" ON PAGE 77. SHOWN AT 100%.

10" (25 CM)

CONNECT HERE

PATTERN USED IN "FABRIC BANNERS" ON PAGE 108. BANNER TOP BORDER 1 INCREASE BY 118%.

**10" (25 CM)**

CONNECT HERE

PATTERN USED IN "FABRIC BANNERS" ON PAGE 108. BANNER TOP BORDER 2 INCREASE BY 118%.

9.75" (24 CM)

CONNECT HERE

PATTERN USED IN "FABRIC BANNERS" ON PAGE 108. BANNER BOTTOM BORDER 1 INCREASE BY 118%.

9.75" (25.7 CM)

CONNECT HERE

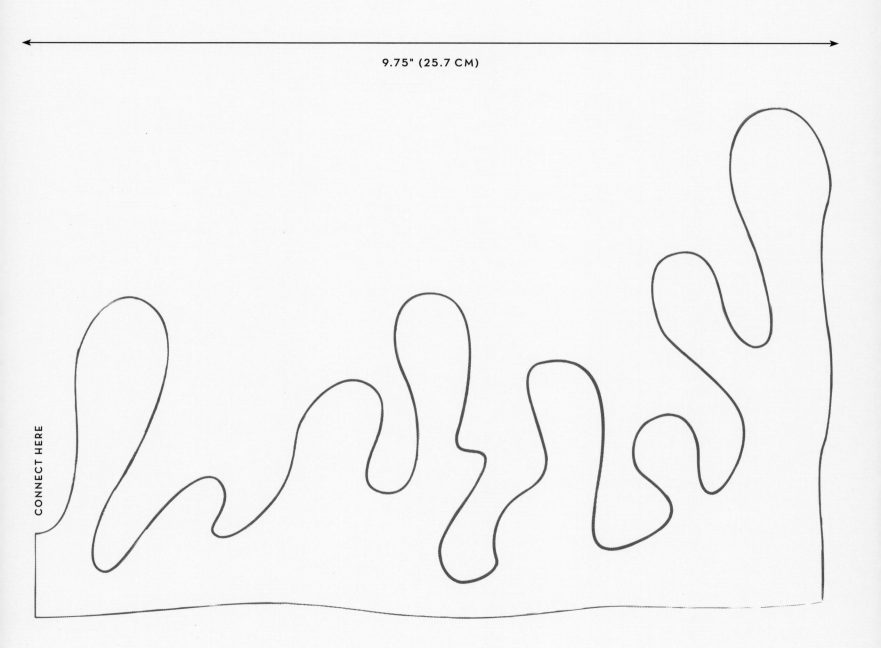

PATTERN USED IN "FABRIC BANNERS" ON PAGE 108. BANNER BOTTOM BORDER 2 INCREASE BY 118%.

**7.75" (19.7 CM)**

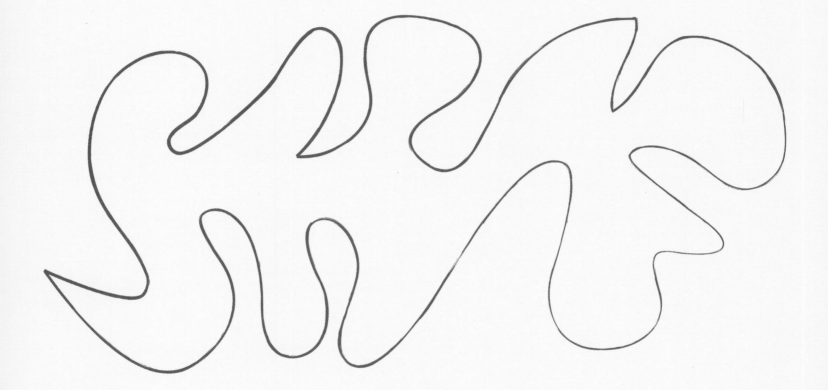

**PATTERNS USED IN "FABRIC BANNERS" ON PAGE 108 AND "LUMINARIES" ON PAGE 109. SHOWN AT 100%.**

6" (15 CM)

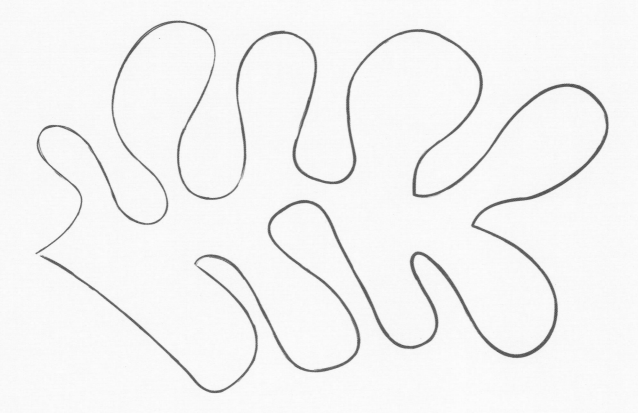

7" (18 CM)

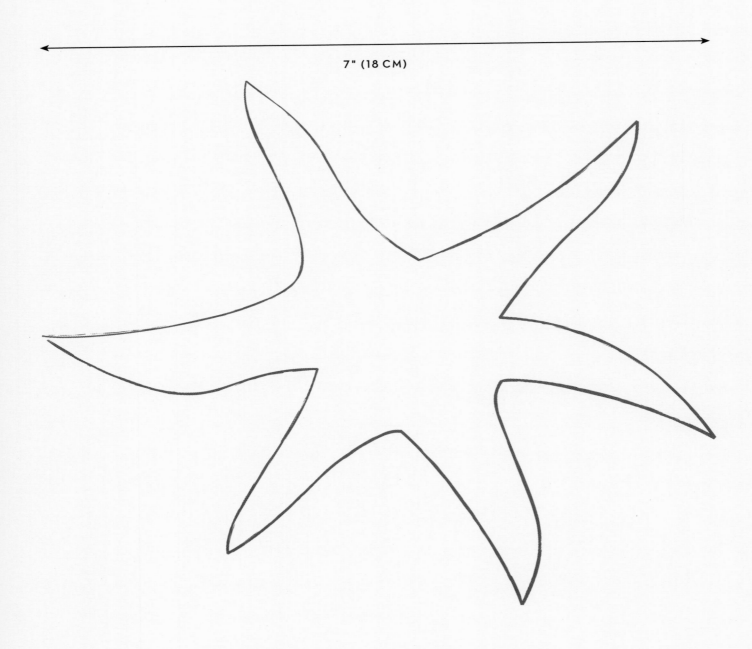

PATTERNS USED IN "FABRIC BANNERS" ON PAGE 108 AND "LUMINARIES" ON 109. LUMINARIES 100%,
BANNERS INCREASE BY 165%.

8" (20 CM)

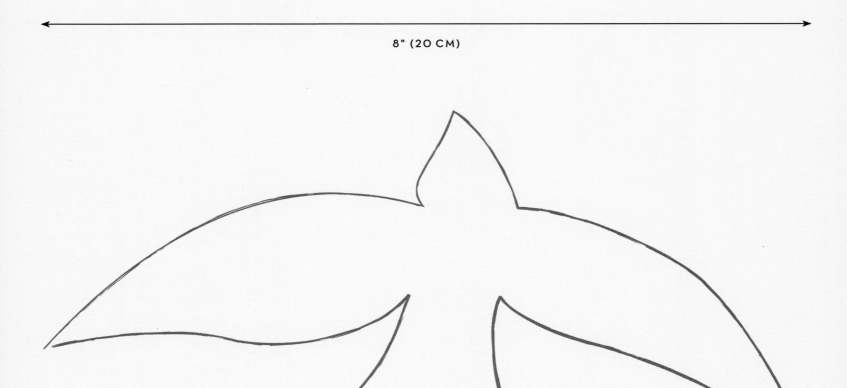

8" (20 CM)

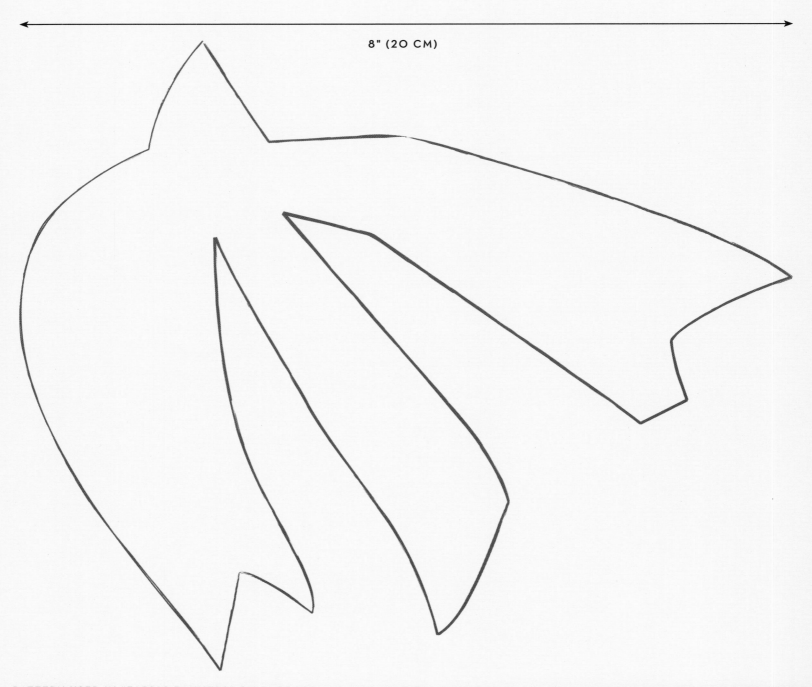

PATTERN USED IN "FABRIC BANNERS" ON PAGE 108 AND "LUMINARIES" ON PAGE 109. LUMINARIES 100%, BANNERS INCREASE BY 165%.

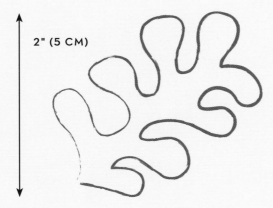

2" (5 CM)

**PATTERN USED IN "EMBROIDERED COCKTAIL NAPKINS" ON PAGE 111. SHOWN AT 100%.**

**PATTERN USED IN "MENU BOARD" ON PAGE 80. SHOWN AT 100%.**

PATTERNS USED IN "STAMPED LINENS" ON PAGE 95. SHOWN AT 100%.

# Chateau Margaux

# GRAND VIN

# 1898

PATTERN USED IN "WINE TOTE" ON PAGE 63. SHOWN AT 100%.

# RESOURCES

*I tend to collect tabletop and kitchenware whenever I see it and can afford it, but there are times when I need the right item right now. In those cases, I always turn to some of my favorite suppliers and friends…*

**Basic French**
5 East Market Street, Red Hook, NY 12571
845 758 0399
WWW.BASICFRENCHONLINE.COM
A sweet little shop offering all sorts of basic items for enjoying the French lifestyle—chocolate, olive oil, baskets, and Côté Bastide china. This shop opened at the same time we opened French General on Crosby Street in New York.

**Dot**
47, rue Saintonge, Paris, France
01 40 29 90 34
WWW.DOT-FRANCE.COM
A small shop, crammed with all sorts of vintage dishes and glassware, that's been a favorite supplier to French General for many years. Stock up while you are in Paris, as the goods are sure to run out sooner or later, and be sure to say hello from Kaari at French General!

**Fishs Eddy**
889 Broadway, New York, NY 10003
212 420 9020
WWW.FISHSEDDY.COM
An emporium of tried-and-true dishes that withstand the test of time! Fishs Eddy is filled with dependable glassware and everyday dinnerware, as well as loads of fun and inspiring vintage pitchers, cake plates, and mugs. When I started writing this book I spent about five hours in this fabulous shop and was given ideas by the smart staff.

**French Basketeer**
WWW.FRENCHBASKETEER.COM
French Basketeer imports authentic French market baskets, rolling carts, and produce bags. They have woven straw baskets in all different sizes, perfect for gathering your fresh food at the farmers' market. My favorite "French"-style baskets are the Aix, Bandol, and St. Paul—all handy for carrying around groceries!

**Goumanyat**
3, rue Dupuis, Paris, France
01 44 78 96 74
WWW.GOUMANYAT.COM
If in Paris, be sure to stop into this amazing gourmet kitchen shop filled with spices, cooking ingredients, and unusual kitchenware. Upstairs is their cookware collection, and downstairs are a wine cellar and a demonstration kitchen. In a city where all I do is eat, this is a neat inside look at the ingredients the French cook with.

**John Derian Company**
6 East 2nd Street, New York, NY 10003
212 677 3917
WWW.JOHNDERIAN.COM
Decoupage doesn't begin to describe the artistry of John's shop. Filled with the odd and unusual, you will be sure to find something unique for your tabletop at this lovely gem of a shop. For textiles, walk fifteen steps east to John's newly opened shop, John Derian Drygoods. Where to next, John?

**The Linen Works**
131 College Road, London, England
44 20 8961 4900
WWW.THELINENWORKS.COM
Beautiful, well-made, practical items for the home. The Linen Works stocks an assortment of good-quality striped ticking fabrics that can be used at the table or in the kitchen. If you don't have the time or energy to make that striped picnic blanket, order a large tablecloth and you are set.

## Maison Midi

148 South La Brea, Los Angeles, CA 90036

323 939 9860

WWW.MAISON-MIDI.COM

A shop and café all rolled into one. Sit and enjoy a light lunch bistro-style, or scoop up café au lait bowls, French damask napkins, and a tin of lavender honey. This is a shop full of Côte Sud inspiration—they even sell the bistro tables and chairs. And if you need the perfect little cardigan for the patio party, just walk through the passageway to American Rag, where you'll find French-inspired clothing galore.

## Petersham Nurseries

Off Petersham Road, Richmond Surrey, United Kingdom

020 8940 5230

WWW.PETERSHAMNURSERIES.COM

Although originally a garden center and café, Petersham Nurseries now stocks wonderful natural linen household textiles, as well as crocks, Ravel pottery, and Astier de Villatte glassware. I've never been to this nursery, but I love browsing their site full of beautiful artisan wares.

## Pierre Deux

3228 Sacramento Street, San Francisco, CA 94115

415 296 9940

WWW.PIERREDEUX.COM

A dependable source for all things French country. Tablecloths, placemats, and napkins all in petite Provençal prints as well as one-of-a-kind wrought-iron chandeliers and rustic farm tables. When I was growing up, Pierre Deux was très chic in our house.

## Posh

613 North State Street, Chicago, IL 60610

312 208 1602

WWW.POSHCHICAGO.COM

One of my very favorite places to find vintage and new French tableware. Karl, the knowledgeable and warm owner, searches high and low for unique items that are rarely seen on dining tables today. Posh stocks it all!

## Rural Residence

316 Warren Street, Hudson, NY 12534

518 822 1061

WWW.RURALRESIDENCE.COM

Rural Residence, an elegant mix of old and new, is located in a wonderful old town called Hudson, which is filled with historical antique shops and restaurants—a great day trip just a short drive north of New York City. The first time I walked into Rural Residence, I thought I had found home.

## Surfas

Corner of West Washington and National Boulevard, Culver City, CA 90232

310 559 4770

WWW.SURFASONLINE.COM

Surfas is a warehouse stocked with thousands of imported and domestic food items, ingredients, and cookware all at discounted prices. A paradise found for serious food enthusiasts and professional chefs. If you live in Los Angeles, this is a must-stop place for 1-pound bags of fresh black peppercorns.

## Sur La Table

WWW.SURLATABLE.COM

A great source for all of your necessary cooking needs, and my favorite place to buy Le Creuset cast-iron pans. I also pick up classic French pepper grinders and picnic knives.

## Napa Vintage

530 574 1618

WWW.NAPAVINTAGE.NET

This online shop is a great source for finding all sorts of authentic French glassware and ceramics. Café glasses, French Périgord stemware, and even Eiffel Tower–stamped water glasses—a different glass shape for every drink.

# INDEX

## ACKNOWLEDGMENTS

· · · · · · · · · · · · · · · · · · · · · · · · ·

Thank you, once again,
to my friends and family who ride this wave
with me when we take on a new project!
In a nutshell (on a beautiful old French cutting board)
thank you kindly to Jody, Molly, Ryan,
Mom, Dad, Sofia, Michael, Jon, and John, Gracie, and
my other John, Dawn, Keith, Horacio,
Brian for the day, Lucy for almost making it,
and finally, Kate, my patient editor,
who lets me do what I do over and over.

··· MERCI. ···